Mr. Bob Peterson
PO Box 126
Veneta, OR 97487

D0392386

We Still Do

We Still Do

CELEBRATING LOVE FOR A LIFETIME

DENNIS & BARBARA RAINEY
GENERAL EDITORS

CONTRIBUTORS:

DENNIS AND BARBARA RAINEY · BOB LEPINE
GARY AND BARBARA ROSBERG · JOSEPH STOWELL
ROD COOPER · CRAWFORD AND KAREN LORITTS
STEVE FARRAR · DAN ALLENDER
TIM AND DARCY KIMMEL · GARY CHAPMAN
GARY SMALLEY

FAMILYLIFE™
Bringing Timeless Principles Home

In honor of the lifelong commitment
to marriage of the parents of
Barbara and Dennis Rainey:

Bob and Jean Peterson
who have celebrated 53 years together

Ward and Dalcie Rainey
who were married 46 years until Ward's death

Contents

1. Uncrumpling a Covenant   3
   Dennis and Barbara Rainey

PART ONE: "I TAKE YOU . . ."

2. Covenant Marriage   11
   Rod Cooper

3. Happiness: The "End Game" in Marriage   25
   Joseph M. Stowell

PART TWO: "TO BE MY HUSBAND OR WIFE . . ."

4. Teamwork in Marriage   41
   Crawford and Karen Loritts

5. Clarifying the "S Word"   53
   Steve Farrar

PART THREE: "TO LOVE, HONOR, AND CHERISH . . ."

6. Speaking Love's Languages 67
Gary Chapman

7. Conflict: Sign of a Normal Marriage 83
Gary and Barbara Rosberg

8. Kill Those Relationship Germs! 97
Gary Smalley

PART FOUR: "TO HAVE AND TO HOLD . . ."

9. God Loves Sex 109
Dan Allender

10. 3-D Sex 123
Tim and Darcy Kimmel

PART FIVE: "'TIL DEATH DO US PART"

11. Marriage for the Glory of God! 139
Bob Lepine

12. Build Your Marriage on the Rock 153
Dennis Rainey

13. Marriage Covenant Memories and Ceremonies 169
Dennis and Barbara Rainey

Small-Group Study Guide 189
Appendix: Your Covenant-Signing Ceremony 205
Notes 209

We Still Do

1

Uncrumpling a Covenant

DENNIS AND BARBARA RAINEY

If you have ever questioned the power of a marriage covenant, you must read what follows.

In fall 2000, during the time period when this book was prepared for publication, we received two letters from a woman we will call Melanie. Except for the alteration of a few minor details to preserve this family's confidentiality, with their permission we share this inspiring story.

Melanie and her husband, Larry, started dating when she was just sixteen. They married seven years later and eventually had three children. From the outside, Melanie and Larry's marriage looked great. They attended a strong evangelical church in a major city and regularly "tuned up" their relationship at marriage conferences. They sought to have a positive influence on other couples and were often described in their circles as the "perfect little family" having the "perfect marriage." But life was not as perfect as it appeared.

Melanie had suspicions about Larry's faithfulness and hired a private detective. To her horror she found out that her husband in fact was having an affair with a woman he had met through his business.

Melanie was crushed, but providentially three days before receiving the sad news, she found a note on her car that read:

Dear Sister in Christ,

Jesus loves you. Praise God for all things!

"For I know the plans that I have for you," declares the LORD, "plans for welfare and not for calamity to give you a future and a hope. Then you will call upon Me and come and pray to Me, and I will listen to you. And you will seek Me and find Me, when you search for Me with all your heart." (Jeremiah 29:11–13)

Melanie clung to that promise from God through her pain and suffering in the following days—during and after her initial confrontation with Larry.

As the weeks passed, Melanie's anger turned to sadness as in reality she mourned the loss of someone she loved. But the anger returned abruptly one night when a discussion with Larry turned into an argument. The two were exchanging verbal blows in their family room where on the wall, surrounded by family photos, hung their nicely framed marriage covenant. In a special ceremony Melanie and Larry had signed the covenant with their three children as witnesses. The kids fully understood what the words of the covenant meant because their parents had reassured them frequently that Mommy and Daddy loved each other and would never get divorced.

During their argument Melanie kept glancing at the marriage covenant. Understandably, the sight of it made her angry. She thought, *He lied to me . . . He promised me that he would always love me . . . He promised he would be faithful.* Finally reaching her boiling point, Melanie jumped up, yanked the covenant off the wall, slammed it on the floor, and screamed: "This means nothing to you! Why did you sign it?" The glass in the frame shattered in a thousand pieces. Melanie picked up the paper covenant and crumpled it.

While this scene unfolded, the children, who had been banished to an upstairs room, heard the tinkling glass and wanted to come downstairs. They were curious about what had happened, but Larry yelled at them to stay away. A sobbing Melanie and her sobered husband swept up the glass and threw the broken frame and covenant in a garbage can.

After this storm, the couple went into another room and continued their discussion in a more civilized manner.

Meanwhile the kids continued to beg. Melanie and Larry relented and the children immediately saw the large blank spot on the wall. Their nine-year-old son, John, in particular, was upset and kept coming to his parents, telling them how bare the wall looked and that something must be done about it. Melanie and Larry reassured him that they would find something to hang there.

A while later John returned and began bugging his mom and dad, saying he needed to show them something. They ignored him for a few minutes, but finally John dragged them into the family room. He pointed to the wall and said, "There, I fixed it!"

Larry and Melanie looked at each other and burst into tears. On the wall hung their battered covenant. John had rescued the crumpled paper from the trash can, smoothed it out, wedged it into the frame, and hung it back on the wall. This boy desperately wanted to fix his parents' marriage and believed that

rehanging their covenant was a good way to start the process. The covenant is still on that wall today—no glass and wrinkled—but it hangs in place.

And John's meaningful intervention did help spur Larry and Melanie into a process of reconciliation.

During some of her most difficult times, a godly friend offered Melanie much encouragement and advice. One time he said, "Go before God and earnestly plead for your family." Melanie did that and said later, "Every time I have wept before God, He has done mighty things. Sometimes I have just wept in confusion, not knowing what to do. Every single time God has been faithful and has clearly shown me what steps to take."

In time Melanie and Larry reached a point of harmony where it was appropriate for Larry to move back home. God continues to change Larry's heart. Not long ago, he once again told Melanie how he couldn't believe he had done this to her and how sorry he was. Larry renewed his promise to do everything possible to get their marriage back on track—and keep it there.

Melanie wrote, "Isn't it awesome how God used this situation to break his heart and move him toward repentance."

And there are three other very happy and thankful members of the family, including young John, who dug a mangled marriage covenant out of the trash and put it back in its rightful place on the family room wall.

That story tears us up every time we read it. How many millions of children in America are trying in their own simple ways to put back together what Mommy and Daddy are breaking? The thought of this grips our heart, but it also recharges our desire to honor and keep our own marriage covenant and help others to do the same.

This book is an overview of the marriage covenant, based on outstanding messages given at FamilyLife's "I Still Do" arena events throughout the United States. We will examine the various sections of the traditional wedding vow and their applications for marriage. Here you will learn what you need to know both about the meaning of a marriage covenant, as well as—most important—how to enjoy the marriage God has given you and make it last a lifetime.

PART 1

"I take you . . ."

Covenant Marriage

Rod Cooper

What is covenant marriage? What does it really mean to have a covenant relationship with the one you love?

As with all good things, the idea of covenant began with God. God's very nature is that of One who makes and keeps covenants. This is revealed emphatically in what I call the Magna Carta of covenants, when God made His special arrangement with Abraham (Gen. 15).

On this occasion, when God gave Abraham the incredible details about his future, we read:

Now when the sun was going down, a deep sleep fell upon Abram; and behold, terror and great darkness fell upon him.

And God said to Abram, "Know for certain that your descendants will be strangers in a land that is not theirs, where they will be enslaved and oppressed four hundred years. But I will also judge the nation whom they will serve; and afterward they will come out with many possessions. And as for you, you shall go to your fathers in peace; you shall be buried at a good old age. Then in the fourth generation they shall return here, for the iniquity of the Amorite is not yet complete." And it came about when the sun had set, that it was very dark, and behold, there appeared a smoking oven and a flaming torch which passed between these pieces. On that day the LORD made a covenant with Abram, saying,

"To your descendants I have given this land,

From the river of Egypt as far as the great river, the river Euphrates." (Gen. 15:12–18)

The phrase *made a covenant* (verse 18) literally means, "God cut a covenant with Abraham." The Hebrew word for *cut* means to sever something from something else by slicing it with a blade. That is why the animals in this incident involving Abraham were split in two. Another requirement of a covenant cutting was that both parties establish their oath by passing between the animal pieces, which showed that blood had been shed and a sacrifice made.

Interestingly, the only one who went through this time was God. In effect He was saying to Abraham, "Let what happened to these animals happen to Me if I don't keep My word. It is unconditional. I will be faithful." To God this was a life-and-death bond—a *covenant*.

With such a dramatic, holy scene revealing the meaning of covenant, how does all of this relate to our marriage covenant? In Genesis 2:24 we find the phrase that helps us understand: "They shall become one flesh." When we enter the covenant of marriage, we take an obligation to our covenant partner. We two become one and are promising in effect that what happened to those sacrificial animals belonging to Abraham will happen to either of us if we don't keep our covenant. And the witness to this holy promise is none other than the covenant-making and -keeping God.

Once you make the marriage commitment, you are in a covenant: the selfless, permanent, interdependent, guaranteed-by-God, unconditional, and mutual relationship. The marriage covenant is not a covenant with an institution; it is a covenant with another person. It is saying, "I take you because God brought you to me."

Enjoying and Preserving a Covenant Marriage

How then can we truly embrace, enjoy, and preserve such a holy, awesome promise as our marriage covenant? Here are four helpful principles.

First, we must realize that our marriage is a reflection of the character of God and not the convenience of our culture.

These days the phrase *your word is your bond* has been

replaced by *contracts were made to be broken*. This attitude slipped into society's view of marriage decades ago. I remember a hit song during the 1970s was Paul Simon's "50 Ways To Leave Your Lover." Today, marriage is considered a merger: If your assets and my assets come together profitably—great. But if your portfolio declines in value, then we will have a downsizing. The result is divorce.

Throughout Scripture we see that marriage is serious business—much more than mergers made to be broken. For example, consider the situation described in Malachi 2. The men living in Judah after the exile were dealing treacherously with their wives; for example, divorcing them over ridiculous things like burning the toast or serving lukewarm coffee. Basically God said to these guys, "When you divorce your wives, guess what? You are divorcing Me as well" (see Mal. 2:14–16).

God takes the oaths that He witnesses very seriously. When the people of Judah asked why He was withdrawing His favor from them, He replied: "Because the LORD has been a witness between you and the wife of your youth, against whom you have dealt treacherously, though she is your companion and your wife by covenant" (Mal. 2:14). God had high expectations for them. He had made these husbands and wives one in flesh and spirit because He was seeking godly offspring from them (verse 15). So, too, for similar reasons we must guard ourselves and not break faith with our spouses.

When we break our bond with each other, we are in a sense implying that God is also failing and not keeping His word. That is why divorce so grieves the heart of God. In

Malachi 2:16, we read, "'For I hate divorce,' says the LORD, the God of Israel." Malachi shows us that a casual attitude toward divorce is a symptom of our heart attitude toward God. Loyalty to Him and to our mate is what counts. Our marriages are a reflection of God's relationship and promises to His people.

When we took our vows we did not say "until an argument do us part" or "until our lawyers do us part" or "until faded passion do us part." Let's face it; if the passion didn't fade, we would all be dead by now! The covenant is not valid only as long as you are attractive or until I have feelings for someone else.

Too often in our narcissistic culture, marriage is like a tick looking for a host. A tick is a parasitic mite that looks for a warm body, like a dog. It latches on and will suck all the blood it can. In contemporary marriage too often we find two ticks and no dog. That's not a covenantal relationship.

Second, your spouse is a gift from God and part of His good plan for you.

You know the story leading up to the original marriage told in Genesis 2. God asked Adam to name all of the animals. While doing this Adam realized how alone he was. The Bible says, "So the LORD God caused a deep sleep to fall upon the man, and he slept; then He took one of his ribs, and closed up the flesh at that place. And the LORD God fashioned into a woman the rib which He had taken from the man, and brought her to the man" (Gen. 2:21–22).

God brought Eve to Adam as a gift. Likewise, your mate is God's gift to you. He has placed in this special person's life all that is good to complement and strengthen you and to help you grow in Jesus Christ.

In my marriage I have found that it is the differences between us that cause the greatest conflicts but also can produce the greatest growth. The truth is, if both people in the marriage are the same, one of them is unnecessary!

My wife, Nancy, and I are complete opposites. I remember shortly after we married that I was looking forward to having breakfast together in the mornings—you know, stimulating conversation, companionship, that sort of thing. Nancy informed me that if God wanted her to see a sunrise, He would videotape it. So much for the cozy breakfast idea!

Not one to give up easily, one morning I waited until Nancy got up, and then I started making breakfast. In my prior bachelor life I would put the eggs in a bowl and beat them with a spoon. This fine morning Nancy walked into the kitchen and asked me what I was doing. "You don't beat eggs. You whisk them," she said. Her expression made me feel like I was committing egg abuse.

"No. I beat eggs," I said.

"Let's be reasonable and do this the right way," she said. "Pour the eggs out and let's start over and do it right."

At that moment we had a very "spirit-filled" discussion on egg beating. (Now that we're mature, Nancy and I don't argue anymore; we just have intense moments of fellowship!) The result was that I no longer beat eggs with a spoon; I use a fork.

We've had tough times that would certainly eclipse egg beating! Knowing that God has given us to each other as gifts, though, has kept us going.

Third, incredible blessings come through covenant marriage.

I receive many personal benefits from my covenant marriage to Nancy: Knowing she won't reject me. Knowing she won't leave me. Knowing she won't try to hurt me. Knowing that I could come to her broken and ashamed and walk away better than I was before.

Such security and safety generate trust. Hebrews 11:17–18 reads, "By faith Abraham, when he was tested, offered up Isaac; and he who had received the promises was offering up his only begotten son; it was he to whom it was said, 'In Isaac your descendants shall be called.'"

Abraham had complete security and safety in his relationship with God because he knew the character of God. He reasoned that if necessary God could raise Isaac from the dead. That's the foundation trust establishes in a marriage.

I've had some days when I really needed my safety and security. At one time, circumstances had left me feeling that I was done with the ministry. We have a basement in our home I call the Cave. My nickname is the Bear; bears go into caves. So in my total frustration and disillusionment, I went downstairs into my cave and began to sob like a baby. No more preaching; no more teaching; no more writing. I was *done!*

Suddenly I felt this hand on my hand. It was Nancy. Now, it takes a brave woman to come into a bear's cave uninvited! Who wants to be mauled by a bear? Nancy is a courageous, straightforward person. She said bluntly, "Rod, I have two things to tell you. Number one, God is on your team. Number two, I'm on your team. If we're on your team, what's the problem? Let's get going."

You know what happened? The Bear ambled out of his cave with a whole new attitude. Sometimes, it's not enough for people to just believe *in* us; they must be willing to believe *for* us. Nancy did that. That is one example of covenant marriage, which says when you can't believe, I'll come alongside and believe for you. That gives amazing security and safety.

Fourth, covenant marriage reveals the power of God and leads others to Jesus Christ.

In America we are hungry for role models. I once asked a boy who he wanted to be like when he grew up. He looked at me and said, "Mister, there ain't nobody that I want to be like when I grow up."

That's tragic.

In the same way that we need good general role models, we also need models of good marriages—unions where people look at us, as they did the early Christians, and say, "Surely this couple has been with Jesus." We need to wear a pin with the phrase *We Still Do* for those times when people approach us and say, "I noticed that when your child got into trouble it didn't split you apart but it brought you together. Why?" Or, "I noticed that when you guys were going through tough financial times, you didn't give up. Why?" Or, "I noticed that when you were having relationship struggles, you and your husband seemed more determined than ever to make it work. Why?"

The answer is, "We still do." We still believe that God will supply our need. We still believe that God will finish what He has begun. We still believe that God has called us together. We still believe that when all you have left is God, God is enough. We still do!

I believe if you embrace these four principles, you won't just endure covenant marriage; you will *love* it.

A Secret to Keeping Your Covenant

If you were to come to our home in Castle Rock, Colorado, you would be treated to two things: a gourmet meal and a dog show.

We have two dogs, Buck and Brandy. They are great, well-trained dogs. Nancy has taught them everything. They can roll over. They can jump in the air. But there is one trick that always amazes me. Nancy will say, "Lay down!" Then she'll take a piece of meat and stick it right on the edge of their noses. She will say "stay," and they'll stay. Those hounds are completely obedient.

I have some fun with this. I walk around provoking those dogs, giving orders like, "Go for it. Enjoy! Get it." Buck and Brandy act like I am not even there. But when Nancy says, "Okay!" the dogs flip the meat in the air and eat it.

This is amazing because a dog's most sensitive spot is his nose. And a dog's greatest desire is to eat meat. So why—even with my urging—do these pets do something so unnatural and obey?

I figured it out, finally. Their eyes never look at the meat; they always stay focused on the master.

There are all kinds of distractions today assaulting covenant marriage, and it is in our nature to want to cut and run. But I have found that those partners whose eyes are on the Master stay put, knowing that it's His approval that counts.

May I be frank? Covenant marriage is an impossible venture! That's why it requires supernatural help. You must be in covenant with the One who makes it possible to keep a marriage covenant. Do that and anything—including covenant marriage—is possible.

Do you have a covenant relationship of your own with God through the shed blood of His Son, Jesus Christ? If not, don't delay! Today is the time to begin a covenant relationship with Him. If you are saying to yourself, "I really want to be in covenant with God by trusting His Son, Jesus Christ," please use the following prayer as a guide to making this decision:

Dear Father, I thank You that You are a God who keeps Your word, and I rejoice in knowing that You don't ask us to do anything that You don't enable us to do. I can't "do" a covenant marriage without a relationship with You. I want to embrace Jesus Christ as my personal Savior. Right now I want to know for sure in my heart that Christ died, cut a covenant, and rose again that I might live. I ask You to give me a fresh start, a new beginning, a second chance. Father, I have sinned. I've tried to live life in my own power. I can't do it. I now place my trust in Jesus Christ as my Savior. Thank You that Jesus died for me and rose again and now can live His life through me. Thank You that I have made covenant with You and that You will never leave me and never forsake me. Thank You for Jesus. In His name I pray. Amen.

If you just prayed that prayer, find another believer soon and tell that person of your decision and your desire to follow Jesus. Ask for prayer and assistance as you begin your covenant relationship with God. If you do not attend a church where Jesus is exalted and obeyed, then make haste to find such a group of fellow believers.

When Jesus enters our life He says, "I take you. I love you. I want to be in covenant with you. I gave Myself for you. Now, let Me live My life through you so you can enjoy what I have for you." The Lord eagerly wants to walk with you in all aspects of life—including your covenant marriage.

Dr. Rod Cooper is a seminary professor, speaker, and author. He and his wife, Nancy, live in Castle Rock, Colorado.

3

Happiness: The "End Game" in Marriage

JOSEPH M. STOWELL

We need to deal with the great American myth that life is supposed to make us happy. This is obviously one of our society's most precious creeds. From television programs to advertisements or just plain ordinary chat on the streets, it is obvious that the supreme personal goal can be summed up in phrases like "Am I happy? Can I be happy? How can I become more happy?"

We need to deal with this perspective particularly when it comes to marriage. My guess is that most of us go into marriage believing that it will make us happy. Or more specifically that the one with whom we have fallen madly in love will guarantee our happiness forever. While a good marriage is a happy one, anyone who has been married for a period of time will tell you that just "being married" does not make one finally and fully happy.

The story of your romance may read something like this: Guy meets girl and suddenly your heart begins to beat more quickly than it has beat in a long time! It's like a knight in shining armor has appeared on the landscape of your life riding on a white stallion. He leans down, swoops you up, puts you on his gallant steed, and you ride off into the sunset. All the while you are thinking, *At last I will be happy. I have found a man who is sensitive and warm. He will listen to me, know all of my needs, and sacrifice all of his interests to meet my needs even when I don't know what my needs are myself.*

He drops the rock. You say yes, and you find yourself at the front of a church. A few months later your expectations have evaporated. Reality sets in. And you are not nearly as happy as you thought you would be.

It is no different for us guys. We fall in love with someone we believe is the most gorgeous woman in the world and think, *She will fix my meals and have my kids. After a hard day at work, she will meet me at the door, hand me the remote control and the newspaper, and tell me to rest in the recliner until dinner is ready. She will feed our bunch of kids and put them in bed. Then she'll spread a linen tablecloth and feed me my favorite meal. After which she will cheerily clean up the dishes while I go back to the TV. And then at eleven o'clock at night she'll slip into a slinky outfit and be a tiger in the bedroom.*

After a few weeks of married life, this myth explodes and you too are not nearly as happy as you thought you would be. So your mind begins to wander: *Since I am not as happy as I thought I'd be, maybe I'll spend more time at work, maybe I'll find a good day-care center and get a career, I'll buy something new, I'll get a boat, we'll get another house, let's have kids, I think I'll have an affair.*

We have to remember that people don't usually have affairs because they are drooling with uncontrolled passion. They usually get sucked into an illicit relationship because they think that at last they have found someone who will make them happy!

These kinds of broken expectations often are the road to a growing bitterness that replaces the fondness we once had toward this one who was supposed to have made us happy.

But before these kinds of thoughts throw us into ultimate despair and disillusionment about marriage, there is a way in which indeed marriage can make one very happy. Happiness in marriage is not found when both partners are devoted to having their other partner provide all the happiness for them. Or to put it more succinctly, happiness in marriage never comes from self-centered behavior. Even a casual glance at the first couple, Adam and Eve, demonstrates that their self-centered responses to life did not bring them joy but took them from the heights of the finest relationship in the world to a life of shame, alienation, and serious family problems (Gen. 3–4).

The bottom line is that happiness is never found in marriage by making front-end demands on our spouses. Happiness instead is the "end game"; it is the result of a good marriage. In other words, if you really want to be happy in marriage, then you have to do marriage the way God intended it to be done, and when that is in process, happiness begins to show up.

So what is the process to which we must be devoted in order to produce what we all want . . . a happy experience with our spouse?

If we were to walk out on the street and ask people what the key is to a great marriage, we would no doubt hear often that four-letter word—*love*. Unfortunately, though, the definition of love is usually quite messed up. To most people the meaning of love is "Am I being loved? Is this person's love making me feel good?"

The Bible, however, expresses quite different thoughts on love and charts the process for what it really means to have a thriving relationship. The Bible uses the Greek word *agape* for our English word *love,* which means "a love that transcends feelings, emotions, and environment." It is a love that loves regardless of what someone else does or doesn't do for me. Agape love is simply that deep-down commitment to be sensitive to, to care about, and to meet the needs of the one you say you love. Agape love involves a willingness to give every resource of our existence to meet the needs of the one we love regardless of circumstances.

For instance in Ephesians 5 the Bible simply says, "Husbands, love your wives." Nothing about feelings there, just do it! Likewise, in Titus, Scripture instructs us on how older women ought to teach younger women to "love their husbands." Not a single reference to happiness. Understanding this is the beginning of how we get to the "end game" of a truly happy marriage. It is imperative that we learn how to be agape-style lovers and get into a covenant-keeping mode.

BECOMING A COVENANT KEEPER

For those of us who are interested in exchanging our belief in the American myth that life should make us happy for something more substantial and enduring, here is a two-step process to bring it about.

Step 1: Get in the Covenant Mode

Once you understand the basics of a marriage covenant, which Rod Cooper ably explained in the previous chapter, you need to apply the covenant mode to your relationship with your spouse. We need to realize that this has nothing to do with your spouse getting in a covenant mode for you. Great marriages always begin with what you can do for your spouse, not what they do for you. So you must acknowledge, "I made a promise; I made a covenant. I am going to keep that promise as God

keeps His promises to me. Regardless of how I feel or am treated, I will be a covenant lover in my home."

It looks like this . . . with a slight exaggeration for emphasis!

Let's say your husband comes home late Friday night. Gobbles down dinner. Then keeps you up late with his romantic demands. In other words all of Friday night is basically about him. He has a tee time the next morning at 8:00 A.M. So as a covenant woman you decide to love him by being aware of his needs and using your resources to meet those needs. So you get up at 6:00 A.M., clean his clubs, rearrange them in the right order, make sure he has enough golf balls, check to make sure his golf glove is in the bag, clean his shoes, and load everything in the car trunk. Then you dust the car off so he can make a presentable entrance at the club.

After doing all of this you head for the kitchen and get the sausage and eggs frying and brew the coffee. About 7:00 you walk into the bedroom and whisper, "Honey, honey! It's time for you to get up. You're playing golf this morning. I've got your clubs and spikes clean. Breakfast is ready. It's right here on this tray. Here's your coffee and fresh squeezed orange juice. Here, let me prop you up. Need a couple of pillows?"

He says, "Wow, wow, you really love me, don't you? Thank you! Thank you!"

And your answer? . . . "Don't thank me. Just remember I'm a covenant woman; that's what is going on here! I'm doing this for Jesus like I'm told to in Ephesians 5:22! And besides, I want to take seriously the proverb that says, 'He who finds a wife finds a good thing, and obtains favor from the LORD' [Prov.

18:22]. To be honest with you, sweetheart, this has nothing to do with you."

Don't say that! But that is exactly what the process is all about. While the details are obviously more than you normally might expect, the reality is that a covenant woman loves her husband for the Lord's sake and for the fact that she is indeed a covenant keeper! Not for what he does or does not deserve.

This principle works on both sides of the street.

Let's say your wife is staying at home to care for your two little children—the youngest being just three months old. After nonstop, 24-7 childcare, she is a very tired woman. One Tuesday night after dinner you reach your hand across the table and say, "Honey, I have a little surprise for you. After we give the children their baths and put them to bed, I want you to take a long soaking bath of your own. Then I insist you crawl into bed with a good book or just go to sleep right away if you feel like it. I—your mighty warrior-husband—will assume the night watch over the children. In fact, I'm going to sleep on the couch so that no sound or stirring will disturb you the whole livelong night! And before I turn in, I'll start the laundry."

If your wife does not need resuscitation at this point, then you administer the loving coup de grâce: "And get this, sweetheart! I have taken a vacation day tomorrow and plan to stay home with the kids. I have already called two of your friends who will arrive at the house at 9:00 A.M. to take you out for breakfast at Omelet Heaven. After that all of you will head for the mall, a movie, and dinner. Oh, and by the way, I put $200 cash in your purse to get a new outfit—you are long overdue for something new and trendy! I'm giving you a twenty-four-hour vacation!"

And she says, "Wow, wow, you really love me, don't you? Thank you! Thank you!"

"Don't thank me!" you say. "Just remember I'm a covenant man, that's what is going on here. I'm taking seriously my need to love my wife like Jesus loves the church [Eph. 5:25]."

For obvious reasons, a wife or husband won't be able to do this very long—or at all—without help! Thus, the next step.

Step 2: Discover the Source of Passion

It's great to want to be a covenant man or woman, but you need more than desire. When you realize you made a covenant before God and many witnesses but all you have are sincere longings, your relationship quickly is going to feel like a big project. You'll get up every morning and have to ratchet up your commitment. You will soon need to ask the question, "Where can I find the motivation to keep this thing going?"

Here's good news. There's a way to turn your covenant commitment from project to passion. It is accomplished through our covenant relationship with Christ. This is actually about inviting a third person into your marriage—Jesus. It is about living in relationship with your spouse as a response to Jesus and not as a response to your spouse.

I find it fascinating that when Christ talks about His relationship with us, He often uses the metaphor of marriage. For example, He referred to Himself as the Bridegroom and to the Church—us—as His bride. This theme was present in subtle ways even when Jesus sought to comfort His traumatized disciples during the Last Supper. That's when He said, "Let not your heart be troubled; believe in God, believe also in Me. In My Father's house are many dwelling places; if it were not so, I would have told you; for I go to prepare a place for you. And if I go and prepare a place for you, I will come again, and receive you to Myself; that where I am, there you may be also" (John 14:1–3).

The exact meaning of those words may fly over our heads, but to these guys sitting around that table, what Jesus told them went deep in their minds and hearts because they knew He was talking about marriage. Let me explain.

To abide by the Jewish marriage customs, if you wanted to marry a Jewish girl, the potential husband went and met with her dad and struck a deal. After the terms were agreed upon, you and the father would seal the agreement as a covenant with the sharing of a goblet of wine. But even though you now had secured a bride, you did not get married the next weekend. You returned to your home and fixed up an apartment for your soon-to-be wife in your father's home.

The really interesting wrinkle was that the girl just had to wait. Unlike today, she did not scurry about planning a wedding. In fact she had no concrete idea when the marriage would occur. It was the groom's responsibility to fix up the couple's new home and make the arrangements for the wedding feast, which was to be held at his dad's home. This process normally took months, sometimes even as long as a year. The bride waited but always had to be ready. She did not know when her bridegroom might come.

Then, one glorious evening the groom would leave his father's home with the wedding entourage, the streets of the village lit by torches. Relatives, friends, and others joined the procession, and the crowd shouted—"The bridegroom is coming! The bridegroom is coming!" The bride would hear the ruckus, run to her window, and then see the torches and throng coming down her street. The covenant that had been sealed with her father long ago was now to become a reality. She would go with her bridegroom back through the streets and enjoy the great wedding feast.

When Jesus said to His disciples, "For I go to prepare a place for you. And if I go and prepare a place for you, I will come again, and receive you to Myself; that where I am, there you may be also," they no doubt remembered fondly many processions and wedding feasts. They knew He was making a

covenant with them that would not be broken. Just think of the comfort this gave them. And Jesus makes the same promise to each of us. He won't break that covenant. You can take it to the bank. Some day, He will return for His own who have believed and trusted in what He accomplished on the cross.

I find it interesting that Christ calls us to think about our marriage in terms of our covenant relationship with Him. So, just as Jesus will keep all His promises to us, He asks that we honor our covenant commitment to our wife or husband for His sake. Just as we are not worthy in ourselves to receive such a blessing from Christ, so our spouse is not always worthy of our love. And if we were to wait until the other person in a covenant commitment was worthy, it would be a long time before we loved them.

Do you see how this level of commitment liberates a marriage? Do you understand why we need the power of our risen Lord present in our marriage? Contrary to the American happiness myth, marriage is not about scheming to get what you want in the relationship. It is about telling Jesus that you love Him enough to love your spouse and to be true to your covenant with him or her because you want to be true to your covenant-keeping Christ.

THE END GAME

So those of us who want a thriving relationship must become wonderfully lost in the reality of a covenant and in the passion of keeping it because of our covenant ties to Christ.

Every time you get to a tense moment in your marriage, you need to take a step back and let your eyes fill with a distant look. Your spouse will ask, "What is going on with you?"

You will answer, "Hang on, I'm just checking in with Jesus about what covenant people do at a moment like this." When you get the answer, pour it on. Just let that love flow! Allow your gratitude to Jesus for what He has done for you, and your willingness to obey Him, drench your partner with kindness, grace, mercy, and love.

You will find that this will become a healing, helping, wonderful step forward in your relationship. And if you try it for two days and it doesn't work, no big deal. You're not doing it for your spouse anyway, are you? You're doing it because of your covenant relationship with Christ because you made a promise to start with. But believe me, in time it will make a difference.

I find it interesting that my wife, Martie, and I can have the most wonderful night and a good morning and our relationship is really tight. I can roll down the driveway, go to work, and have the worst day imaginable. It can be absolutely in a ditch all eight hours. But life still is okay because in my heart everything is good at home.

The flip side is true as well. If Martie and I are out of sync and it is terrible at home, I can have the best possible day at work, but life is not all that good. Because down in my heart I have this deep ache about what is going on in my marriage.

We need our relationships to thrive at home if we are to be happy. But that happiness is only possible when we keep the covenant through the power of Christ.

You really can be happy and married. Bask in the blessings of making and living out this covenant of love.

Dr. Joseph Stowell is president of Moody Bible Institute, a radio show host, and author of several books including his latest, Loving Christ. *He and his wife, Martie, live in Chicago.*

PART 2

"To be my husband or wife . . ."

4

Teamwork in Marriage

CRAWFORD AND KAREN LORITTS

We said, "I do," on a sunny spring day in May of 1971 at Memorial Baptist Church in Philadelphia. We had written our own vows and pledged our hearts to one another. And in one of Karen's vows she made a promise to submit to her husband.

After the ceremony we were standing outside the church in the receiving line and we overheard someone grumble, "She must be out of her mind to promise to submit to some man!"

We know many people today would say the same thing because there's much confusion in our world about roles and relationships in marriage. We have trouble understanding what a life-long commitment to marriage is all about. Who are we as husband and wife? What are we supposed to do? What is our assignment?

What is our responsibility? Can't we just room together? You do your part, I do my part, and everything will be hunky-dory? Can't we define and maintain some sort of fifty-fifty relationship?

To add insult to injury, we're living in a culture in which men don't understand what a man should be, and increasingly women are not affirmed in what it really means to be a woman. And so we bring a lot of role confusion into a marriage. In addition, we do not marry just the person we love; we marry their history, for good or bad, all of their positive and negative traits, the great experiences as well as the horrendous stresses and dysfunctions that plague us all. Unless we have some type of objective criteria to describe, define, and determine the parameters of our relationship, we will collide and possibly divorce. Or we will allow the relationship to dissolve into some type of "peaceful coexistence" when we ought to have a mind-set of complementing and completing one another.

How can we experience wholeness and a sense of identity, direction, and completeness in our marriage relationship? What does God say are the boundaries that will help make this happen? We need to go back to what Scripture says about our assignment and not necessarily what the culture, the talk shows, and the magazines tell us. First Crawford will share some thoughts for a husband, and then Karen will do the same for a wife.

The Husband's Job Description

Some years ago a young couple came to my office for some counseling. I don't think I have ever met two stronger people in my life. They had been married about six months and were at each other's throats. It was absolutely awful; they were even shouting at each other while they came into my office.

"Whoa, whoa, whoa, whoa!" I said. "Wait a minute. What's the problem?"

The man kept saying, "She won't submit to me!"

His wife looked pretty tough, so I said to her, "Would you step out of the room for a minute?"

After the door closed I said, "Man, what's the deal?"

"She just won't submit to me," he said, still mighty agitated.

"Hold it. Calm down, buddy," I said. "Now you have a couple of problems here. First, she looks awfully strong, and I'm not so sure you want to push this. What are you going to do—beat her up?" (I wasn't being terribly spiritual, but just using common sense—I was thinking about this guy, *Your dog doesn't stand a chance in that fight, pal.*)

Then I asked him, "Whose problem is it that she won't submit?" Not taking any risks I immediately answered my own question: "It's not your problem. Your job is to work on giving her something to submit to. Her obedience to God or response to you is not your responsibility. That's hers. But what you need to do is clearly outlined in Ephesians 5—the job description of every husband."

There is really only one responsibility in that Ephesians job description, one enormous responsibility. It's almost as if the apostle Paul reaches out, grabs men by the lapels, and says, "Husbands, love your wives just as Christ loved the Church." That's it.

Leadership in the Bible has nothing to do with rank. It's not your title but what you *do* in your position. Positions are given as a platform for service—ways to express the servant leadership of our Savior.

In New Testament times it was a common custom for the lowest of the slaves to wash the feet of the invited guests (in much the same way that today we give our invited guests a glass of cold water or iced tea). The day that Jesus arrived at the house where He would eat His last supper, there were evidently no servants available. Modern management paradigms would suggest that because He was the CEO, Jesus should have delegated the foot washing to one of the employees. He could have said, "Peter, James, John, Andrew, Bartholomew—one of you get a basin of water and a towel and wash feet. I need to put My message together."

No, Jesus, the Lord of history, the One who had created those disciples, the One who had created the water, the One who created everything, got down on His knees and said in effect, "Gentlemen, I'm going to teach you a lesson in leadership that you'll never forget."

Leadership in the home has nothing to do with having *Mr.* in front of our names or intimidating and bullying people. It has nothing to do with the remote control or the easy chair. It has everything to do with showing the desire to outserve anybody who's in the house.

Love Her Sacrificially

Loving our wives as Christ loved the Church is first expressed as we love our wives sacrificially. Paul writes, "Husbands, love your wives, just as Christ also loved the church and gave Himself up for her" (Eph. 5:25).

We husbands need to give ourselves to helping our wives be great. A woman does not become a wife just to wash our dirty underwear, pick up after us, make sure we look good, and get us to appointments on time. We should be committed to supporting and encouraging *them*. Think about what Jesus did for the Church. He died on the cross in our place and for our sins. He's the One who said about us who would follow, "Greater works than these shall you do because I go to the Father." One of those great works is to help our wives be successful.

My love and commitment to my wife should include everything I know God has for that woman. I don't want to stand in the way of His plans for her growth and well-being. I want to be her number one cheerleader. I want to translate God's vision for her into reality. I want to empower her. I want to make sure that every roadblock, every barrier, every obstacle that stands in the way of her fulfilling God's mission is pushed aside.

I want Karen to outshine me in every category. When people look at me, I want them to think of Karen.

Another part of sacrificial love is the husband giving himself exclusively to his wife. Christ gave Himself up for His bride, the Church, that He might sanctify her. The word *sanctify* means "to be set apart." Jesus wants an exclusive relationship with a beautiful, pure bride, which the apostle Paul described as "having no spot or wrinkle or any such thing; but that she should be holy and blameless" (Eph. 5:27).

Jesus has only one bride. Jesus does not have an *affair* with anything or anybody else. He is a *one-woman* man. That's the model for us in marriage.

Love Her Attentively

Here is another aspect of the job description Paul gives to husbands. In wrapping up this thought, he says in Ephesians 5:28, "So husbands ought also to love their own wives as their own bodies." That word *ought* is a contraction of two words. It's an old English word meaning "owe" and "it." It is a statement of obligation. Paul is saying, "Men, when you said, 'I do,' you did." When you make a promise on your wedding day, God says you have the job. And now that you two have become one, that means more than the sexual union. You now have a responsibility to take care of that woman in the same way you take care of yourself.

According to Paul's job description, this servant-leader in the house, this translator of vision to reality, this one who empowers people around him, nourishes his wife mentally and spiritually. He helps her, invests in her, and cherishes her. He doesn't abuse, neglect, or take advantage of her. She is his precious jewel.

WHAT SUBMISSION MEANS TO KAREN

Crawford and I have been married twenty-nine years, and I still remember the wedding ceremony as though it were yesterday. I was nervous trying to memorize those vows and say them just right. But I did it. I stood and looked at Crawford in front of my pastor and my whole family and said I would love, honor, cherish, obey, and submit to him. And I meant every word. I wanted our relationship to be another testimony of what God was doing in my life.

After the ceremony we had a nice reception and then got into our little car and drove away for a four-day honeymoon trip. Three day days later I was in the bathroom looking in the mirror and broke out in a cold sweat. I was scared. I realized that I was going to have to live with this guy twenty-four hours a day, seven days a week, month after month, year after year. Sure, I had meant my vows. I loved Crawford. God had given him to me miraculously. But I was afraid now to come off this honeymoon mountaintop to go down and live with the man.

Crawford came from a family where his mom and dad had been married almost fifty-three years before they went home to be with the Lord. A perfect little family. A great mom who loved and served her husband and her children. A father who was the man of the home and a great leader.

I came from a single-parent family; I was born to an unwed teenage girl. We were poor and on welfare a while. Men were an endangered species in my mother's family; they didn't stay around long. The women usually didn't get married and those who did stayed married for only a short period of time before pushing the men out the door. My mother modeled to me that men will do you wrong. They will not be there for you. You need to be self-sufficient. You depend upon yourself.

That was my background; so now as a newly married woman I was scared. Could we make it as husband and wife coming from such completely different backgrounds? Was I really prepared to be a wife?

But I was a Christian. I knew that made all the difference. God had come into my life at age fourteen and miraculously saved me. I could always go back to the one Person who never changed. And that was Jesus.

And so at that crucial point on my honeymoon I remembered a verse in Proverbs that says, "He who finds a wife finds a good thing, / And obtains favor from the LORD" (18:22). I knew I was not yet that good thing for Crawford. I did not know what it meant to be a wife. So I cried out in prayer in that bathroom and asked, "God, You are an unchanging God. You are a sovereign God. And I need You right now to live Your life through me, and to teach me what it means to really love this man that You have given me. Help me to be that gift to him."

We ended the honeymoon and my life started to change. God took control and helped me in my marriage.

One of my responsibilities was in the area of submission to Crawford. Up to this point, I had thought *submission* was a dirty word. I had always heard women or even preachers talk about submission in a way that made it sound like the wife was the lesser of the two partners in a marriage. Husbands were depicted as dictators, and wives were described like doormats.

But I concluded, *No, that can't be from the God I know.* "Lord," I prayed, "I want You to tell me and show me from

Your Word what it means to submit to my husband." I ended up in Ephesians 5 and Colossians 3. I finally learned what submission really is.

God said, "Karen, to be submitted to Crawford, first you need to be yielded to My will." I knew that in Proverbs it said to "trust in the LORD with all your heart, / And do not lean on your own understanding. / In all your ways acknowledge Him, / And He will make your paths straight" (Prov. 3:5–6).

"God, make my path straight," I asked. I knew I could trust God because years earlier He had rescued my life when I was headed to a dead end. Certainly now, as a married woman, He could make my new path straight.

I also learned that I needed to commit myself to God's established order for the family. God is wise, and He devised this plan and instituted marriage. My husband is my designated head. He is to be my servant-leader. We wives are to come alongside and complete our husbands—to fill in those gaps where they need us. So my responsibility was to come alongside Crawford, not to be a doormat or his punching bag or to blindly obey him, but to love, support, and submit to him.

Another truth God taught me about submission was that I needed to learn how to be an aggressive follower. Those of us who are high controllers need to realize that God knows better than we do how to run things. He wanted to unclench my grip so that He could put blessings into my open hands. I needed to learn how to be a follower of Jesus first and then of my husband.

Last, God said that those who submit must lead a disciplined life. I needed to learn how not to let my mouth run away with me. I used to say the wrong things at the wrong time and respond not so lovingly toward Crawford. I wasn't full of grace and mercy. I needed a powerful God working in my life. Submission for me has become something that I do through the power of the Holy Spirit.

This often isn't easy, but I've seen God faithfully shape and mold my life. And the obedience of my submission has become a testimony to my family. Every time they come through our front door, they know that Jesus is the reigning Person in our home and that I love and submit to Crawford. I see them being drawn to Jesus because they know if He can change Karen's attitudes and life, then Jesus can do anything.

At the end of our wedding ceremony, Crawford sang a song with words that said, "Savior, like a Shepherd lead us, much we need Thy tender care." I often still hear that song playing in my mind, and I pray: "Lord, we want You to lead because we do need Your tender care."

Dr. Crawford and Karen Loritts live in Atlanta, Georgia, and are the parents of four children. Crawford is an author, speaker, radio host, and Associate U.S. Director for Campus Crusade for Christ. Karen, on staff with Campus Crusade for twenty-three years, is a conference speaker and Bible study teacher. She also serves on ministry and foundation boards.

5

Clarifying the "S Word"

STEVE FARRAR

I remember the reaction when I first found out that I had been chosen to give the message at an "I Still Do" event on how a husband and wife need to complement each other in their respective marital roles. Some of my fellow-speaker buddies started kidding me: "Hah, Farrar, you get to do 'the talk'! You get to speak about *submission!*"

I knew their jibes were good-natured, but the fact that any discussion of male and female roles in marriage—even among Christians—creates such a buzz is revealing. Why should a discussion of ideas so clearly presented in the Bible spark such controversy? My friends would not have teased me if my assigned message were on the Trinity or the meaning of the Cross.

Of course, the reason why the topic of roles in marriage stirs such passion is that our culture has changed. Thirty years ago, almost nobody would have questioned what I am about to share from the Word of God about marriage. God's Word hasn't changed, but the culture's values have.

If this subject confuses and troubles you, I urge you to set aside your preconceptions and prejudices and pay careful attention to what the Scriptures say. I will present the biblical data as clearly and concisely as possible. Then you can decide prayerfully what conclusions to reach based on this evidence. Regardless of the pressures from our culture, we must obey God in all things—including how we relate in a covenant marriage.

EQUAL BUT DIFFERENT

I would rather not admit this, but one day I was driving at about 58 mph in a 35 mph zone. A guy pulled up behind me. He had two features on his car that I didn't have on mine: a siren and a red light. Both were turned on.

I looked in the mirror and thought, *Who does he think he is? He is no better than I am. We're both equal under the Constitution. We're both equal under the Bill of Rights. We're both citizens. Who does he think he is?*

This guy behind me may have agreed with these thoughts, but since he happened to be a police officer, he needed to do his duty and get me in line. Were we equal as citizens and before God? Absolutely! But in that situation, the man in uniform had obvious authority over me. And for my own good I needed to submit to him.

The issue of authority is crucial to an understanding of roles in relationships. If as Christians we do not accept the truth that we are under the authority of God and others, then concepts like male headship and female submission in marriage will not mean much. Whether you are male or female, if you do not submit yourself to the authority of God and His Word, you are not walking in the steps of Jesus, the apostles, and the saints of all ages. Jesus told us the way it is for everyone: "All authority has been given to Me in heaven and on earth" (Matt. 28:18).

In fact, we do practice authority in every area of life. In order for society to function without anarchy and chaos, somebody has to possess and exert authority. In every endeavor we practice authority among equals: Someone has to follow; someone has to lead. It doesn't mean that the follower is the lesser. At your work you probably have some people under you who follow your direction. But you also probably have someone over you.

But authority does not obliterate another key truth taught in Scripture—equality. Man and woman are equal in the sense that they bear God's image equally. We both stand before God bearing His image—male and female.

In the account of Creation, God said, "'Let Us make man in Our image, according to Our likeness; and let them rule over the fish of the sea and over the birds of the sky and over the cattle and over all the earth, and over every creeping thing that creeps on the earth.' And God created man in His own image, in the image of God He created him; male and female He created them" (Gen. 1:26–27).

God's Word says so. That settles it. Men and women are equal.

But equality doesn't mean sameness. God created men in His image. God created women in His image. God wants men to be masculine. God wants women to be feminine. Today's culture seems to have a problem with this basic truth and tries to blur the distinctions between male and female. But He created us different. God likes the difference. In fact, He delights in it.

And equality does not mean that the equals will always possess equal authority. Going back to my little incident with the police officer, for the protection and peace of society, that man had been given authority over a citizen like me—even though as human beings we were of equal value.

By His wisdom, and for the good of us all, this is what God

also did in other societal and personal relationships—including the home: He established an authority structure that placed the man in headship over the woman and, in turn, the man and woman exert authority over their children. Both man and woman remain under the authority of God and must submit to Him.

Yes, there it is—the much-maligned "S word": *submission*.

But submission is not just an issue for women. Every one of us who seek to obey and follow Jesus needs to understand what the Bible says about the "S word." Jesus Himself submitted to the Father: "My Father, if it is possible, let this cup pass from Me; yet not as I will, but as Thou wilt" (Matt. 26:39). James wrote specifically to us, "Submit therefore to God" (James 4:7).

But in the covenant of marriage between two spiritually equal human beings, the man has been given authority and bears the primary responsibility to lead the marriage in a God-glorifying direction. That is God's plan for marriage.

Before going on, I do want to debunk a myth that says the Bible and Christianity put women down. That idea is theologically and historically untrue. As I've already shown, the Bible teaches true equality between men and women. And the record shows that wherever Christianity has gone in the world, the status of women has gone up.

Some years ago in India, when Prime Minister Gandhi was assassinated, they took his body and put it on a wooden raft on the Ganges River. They covered his body with kindling wood and flowers and said the appropriate words. At the end of the service, they put a torch to that wooden raft, and his body was cremated.

Did you know that in the past they would have taken the dead man and done the same things, but before lighting the torch, they would have placed the man's very-much-alive wife on the pyre and sent her to a horrible death by burning? It was that way in India for thousands of years before the truth of Jesus Christ arrived there. Then the practice was stopped. Similar changes have always occurred wherever the truth of

Christ has spread, because where Jesus and His followers go, the status of women rises.

THE BIBLICAL CASE FOR MALE HEADSHIP

God's basic structure for the male-female relationship was established at the very beginning. In the Creation account in Genesis 2, we read, "Then the LORD God formed man of dust from the ground, and breathed into his nostrils the breath of life; and man became a living being. And the LORD God planted a garden toward the east, in Eden; and there He placed the man whom He had formed" (2:7–8).

So far, so good. Since man was alone, there was no need yet for advice on relationships! The story continues later in this chapter of Genesis: "And out of the ground the LORD God formed every beast of the field and every bird of the sky, and brought them to the man to see what he would call them; and whatever the man called a living creature, that was its name" (verse 19).

Keep in mind that when Adam was assigning names to all the beasts and birds, he was still alone. In the Old Testament and on to our day, the ability to name something is a ruling function. As parents we name our children. We don't wait until the kids are eighteen and then let them pick out their own names. We assign names to them after birth because parents have authority over their children. Adam named the animals as God brought them to him, because he had been given authority by God over the creation.

But now the plot thickens: "And the man gave names to all the cattle, and to the birds of the sky, and to every beast of the field, but for Adam there was not found a helper suitable for him" (verse 20).

Just imagine what this was like: Adam is just Adam. He shows up every day for work at the Garden and punches in. He's never read Genesis. Boom, he had been created and now is seeing all this stuff, but he has this empty spot in his life—he probably doesn't even know the word for it—*need*. He is alone and doesn't know what is going on.

As these different animals come to him, he sees a pattern: male, female, male, female, one corresponding to the other. Adam is looking and begins to wonder—Will one show up like me? But nothing promising appears. The hippo comes along, and Adam says, "No way!"

Here is what happened. "So the LORD God caused a deep sleep to fall upon the man, and he slept; then He took one of his ribs, and closed up the flesh at that place" (verse 21).

So God took a rib, fashioned the woman, and then brought her to Adam. And Adam said the equivalent of, "All right! Yes, Lord. Thank You, Jesus!" He looked at her. This was no giraffe. This was no peacock. This was good. And Adam said, "This is now bone of my bones, / And flesh of my flesh; / She shall be called Woman, / Because she was taken out of Man" (verse 23). And then this part of the story concludes, "For this cause a man shall leave his father and his mother, and shall cleave to his wife; and they shall become one flesh. And the man and his wife were both naked and were not ashamed" (verses 24 and 25).

A few verses before this the Bible explains how God had known Adam would need a partner: "Then the LORD God said, 'It is not good for the man to be alone; I will make him a helper suitable for him'" (verse 18). So now God has completed His work and Adam has a mate, which He called a *helper*.

Some people look at that word and say, "That's a depreciating term." The wife is a *helper*? Yes. The man was not created functionally to help the woman, although in loving her he certainly helps her. But the point is that the Word of God says she was created to assist and complete him. In Scripture, *helper* is not a demeaning term because it is even used to refer to God Almighty Himself. God relishes helping us. The third person of the Trinity, the Holy Spirit, is called our helper.

A theology being taught in some Christian colleges says the spiritual headship of a husband is the result of sin, and that God's real plan before the Fall was not for men to be the spiritual leaders of their family. That teaching may play well in contemporary culture, but it is not what the Word of God teaches. There are several facts that support male headship.

The first is that man was created first. There is a principle in the Old Testament called *primogeniture,* which means that the one who was first born had authority over the others. In this instance the man, who came before the woman, has the rights of primogeniture.

Second, when the man was still alone, he was given the responsibility of naming all the creatures, which was a ruling function. As a result man named the woman because in this relationship of equals, he was given authority and designated the leader.

Finally, the woman was created to be a helper suitable for the man and not vice versa. As I explained already, that is not a put-down. It just means the two are to have different roles and will complement one another.

The pattern of male headship is reinforced in the New Testament as well. As Crawford and Karen Loritts have already explained so well in this book, the apostle Paul drew a parallel between Christ's commitment to the Church and a husband's to his wife. In Ephesians 5:23, he stated plainly, "For the husband is the head of the wife."

If you are a wife who has been hurt through a husband's domination and refusal to function according to God's blueprint, no doubt you will find it hard to accept this truth. A man can absolutely abuse his authority. Let me make it very clear that male headship is *not* male domination. If we miss this point, we're going to miss the whole concept.

We see horrible abuses of women in our culture and even in the Church. But remember, male headship is not male dominance. However, we must not throw the baby out with the bath water. These are God's ideas.

I pastored for fifteen years and saw and heard all kinds of viewpoints related to this topic. Some men came to see me, claiming they were the spiritual leaders of their homes. That was a lie. Instead, they were the "spiritually out-of-control controllers" in their homes. I once heard a wife say, "He won't let me make a phone call without his permission." I looked at her husband and said, "Look, you are the husband, not the Holy Spirit. And guess what? You're not even the Holy Spirit's assistant!"

God has said both male and female are made "in My image." They are equal before Him. But in order for this marriage covenant to function, one is to lead and one is to follow. That's His game plan for the family. This covenant that we call marriage is very, very dear and very, very special to Him. Just because it is distorted in our day does not mean it's not right or true.

If you are a husband, I challenge you to carry your headship with grace, honor, and tenderness in your family. You should be the example in your home of submission to the authority of God, your employer, legal authorities, and leaders of your church. You should be the one who demonstrates by what you say and do what it means to be in submission to the Word of God.

Likewise, if you are a wife, I challenge you to carry out your submission with grace, honor, and tenderness in your family. You should be the example in your home of submission to the authority of God, your husband, your employer if you work, legal authorities, and leaders of your church. Your children will learn from you what it means to submit gracefully in the family setting.

SEEK GROWTH, NOT PERFECTION

Is living out our assigned roles hard? Absolutely! Do we always get it right? Nope! My wife, Mary, and I certainly don't.

We know though that this is a process and we have time; in a covenant marriage we're not going anywhere else. Sometimes we have conflict on this topic, but we keep working on it and trying to develop harmony. And how does a married couple develop harmony? By practicing. If you want to play the piano, you must practice. So harmony in marriage also requires practice.

Mark Twain once said he could live sixty days on a good compliment. One day Mary and I will both stand before the Lord Jesus Christ. You know what we want to hear from Jesus? We want Him to look at us and say, "Steve, Mary, well done in your marriage."

That's a compliment that won't carry us for just sixty days, but throughout eternity.

Dr. Steve Farrar is founder of Men's Leadership Ministries. He is the author of Point Man: How a Man Can Lead His Family, Anchor Man, Get in the Ark, *and other books. Steve and his wife, Mary, reside in Texas and are the parents of three children.*

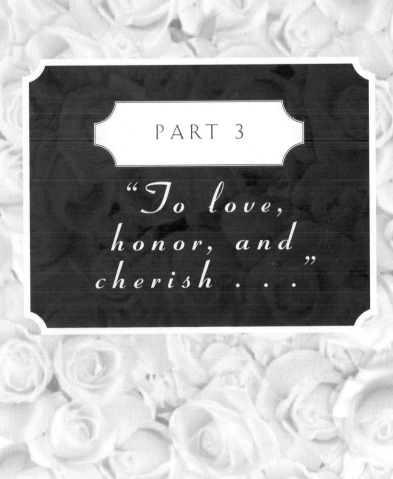

PART 3

"To love, honor, and cherish . . ."

6

Speaking Love's Languages

GARY CHAPMAN

No one ever forgets the *tingles*.

For the guy, the *tingles* may have hit the day he was in the hallway at school and she came out of class and he thought, *Oooh, must be a transfer student. I have never seen her before. I don't even know her name.* But he already felt the *tingles*.

For the girl, the *tingles* may be the first time she saw him in a football uniform. He looked so strong. "Where did he come from?" she asked her friend. "Do you think he noticed me? I hope so!"

I call that little experience the *tingles*. It's the tingles that motivate us to ask someone out.

Sometimes you lose the tingles on the first date. You find out your love interest dips snuff and the tingles vanish. But with another person, the first time you have a hamburger you can hardly wait to have another hamburger. And it gets tinglier and tinglier, until one night when the moon is right, one of you says: "You know, I think I love you."

That's called *testing the waters*. You want to see if this special friend is feeling what you are feeling. And if he or she gives you a positive response, the next time the moon is right, one of you will actually say, "I love you." And if the response comes, "I love you too," then you know this is now a more advanced stage of tingles.

From that point on, you get obsessed with each other. You can't get this most wonderful person off your mind. You go to bed thinking about him. You wake up thinking about her. All day long—you can't focus on anything else.

Now, your mother may see flaws, but you can't. She will say, "Darling, have you considered that Mr. Fantastic hasn't had a steady job in three years?"

And you reply, "Mama, give me a break; he's just had bad luck. He's going to make it."

Dorothy Tennov of Bridgeport, Connecticut, did a long-term study on the "in love obsession." She discovered that the average life span of this obsession is two years. So it takes just about twenty-four months to come off the high.[1]

We should thank God we don't stay obsessed forever. If we did, business, industry, the Church—all of society would have to close down. You can't get anything done when you are in love!

I'm not putting down the *falling in love tingles*. It's a wonderful experience! The temporary tingles are just not a good foundation for marriage. So what can we do when the tingles subside, and we realize that Mama may have been right about some things?

The Five Languages of Love

After almost thirty years of marriage and family counseling, I am convinced there are five basic ways to express love emotionally. I call these the five love languages. Of course there are many nuances or *dialects* of these languages, which I discuss in depth in my book *The Five Love Languages* (Northfield Publishing, 1995). This overview will explain how they enhance a marriage.

Language 1: Words of Affirmation

In Scripture we read that "love edifies" (1 Cor. 8.1). Love builds up its recipient. Some people need this kind of verbal encouragement more than others. So to love them we must use words that build them up. Let me explain.

If you are a wife, your husband has hopefully said something like this to you in the last week: "You look nice in that dress."

If you are a husband, perhaps your wife has said something like: "Oooh, do you ever look good tonight."

So many women come to my office and say, "I give it everything I've got, but he never says a positive word. All he does is criticize."

I also hear many men say, "I don't ever get any words of affirmation. I get out there and bust myself all day long, and she never says a positive word."

Do you see why the Bible says, "Death and life are in the power of the tongue" (Prov. 18:21)? We can give life with our words. An incredible way to express love is through positive affirmation.

Language 2: Gifts

It is a universal truth that giving gifts is an expression of love. The best-known verse in all the Bible is John 3:16: "For God so loved the world, that He gave His only begotten Son." As a result, through Jesus we receive the gift of eternal life.

God is a gift giver, and if we love, we give gifts too. They don't need to be expensive. Don't we often say, "It's the thought that counts"? But it is not the thought left in your head that counts; it is the *gift* that results from the thought!

If you are a husband, go pick a flower for your wife. If you don't have one in your yard, go ask if you can pick one of your neighbor's!

If you are a wife, rummage through his closet and find something you know he can use but has forgotten that he has. Wrap it up and present it with fanfare. If he recognizes it, so what! It is still a gift and you get emotional credit!

Gifts are concrete expressions of love.

Language 3: Acts of Service

The apostle John wrote, "Let us not love with word or with tongue, but in deed and truth" (1 John 3:18). Do something to show your love.

Cooking a meal is an act of service. You remember the old saying "The way to a man's heart is through his stomach"? There is some truth to that. And a similar truth is that the way to a woman's heart is through the restaurant door!

Who takes the pizza box out at your house? That's an act of service. Vacuuming floors, rubbing the white spots off the mirror, putting gas in the car, changing the baby's diaper . . . the list is endless. Do something!

Language 4: Sharing Quality Time

Jesus demonstrated this with His disciples. He chose twelve men and set them apart "that they might be with Him, and that He might send them out to preach" (Mark 3:14). Jesus preached to the multitudes, but He gave quality time to twelve friends.

This principle applies to any relationship. By quality time, I mean giving the other person your undivided attention.

In a restaurant have you ever noticed how you can usually tell whether a couple is dating or married? Dating couples look at each other and talk. Married couples often just eat.

Quality time is not achieved sitting together on the couch watching television. Then Madison Avenue and the networks have your undivided attention. Instead, sit on the couch with the TV *off*.

If I sit on the couch with my wife for twenty minutes and look and listen and interact, I have given her twenty minutes of my life and she has done the same for me. What a powerful message of love!

Language 5: Physical Touch

There is great emotional power in physical touch. When little children were brought to Jesus, the disciples essentially said, "Get rid of these kids. Can't you tell? Jesus is too busy for kids." What did Jesus say? "Permit the children to come to Me; do not hinder them; for the kingdom of God belongs to such as these" (Mark 10:14). Later it says that He put His hands on them and blessed them (verse 16). We can bless others with our touch. That's why we pick up babies, cuddle them, and say all those silly words.

In marriage this means holding hands, kissing, embracing,

sexual intercourse, running your hand through your lover's hair. There's loving power in your touch.

What's Your Love Language?

Out of these five love languages, one is more important to you than all the others. You may like all of them, but if you had to give up all but one, you would keep your primary one. This is the one that when your spouse uses it, you really feel loved.

Occasionally someone says to me, "I don't know. I think two of these languages are just about equal for me."

My answer is, "Fine. We'll give you two love languages. We'll call you bilingual." But most of us have a primary love language, a secondary love language, and the other three fall in line after them.

A husband and wife almost never have the same love language. And by nature we speak our own language; this means whatever makes you feel loved will be what you tend to do for your spouse. But if that is not his or her primary language, it will not communicate the same meaning it has for us.

A pastor once told me that he had realized after many years of marriage that he and his wife had not been speaking each other's primary love language. The man commented, "My wife's language is gifts, and my language is words of affirmation. For years my wife gave me gifts. My closet was full of stuff I never used. I said to her along the way, 'Why do you keep bringing home all this stuff?' For seventeen years I gave her words of affirmation. I told her how good-looking she was. I told her what a good mother she was. Sometimes I poured it on so strongly that my wife said to me, 'Would you please knock it off.' What she meant was, 'Cut the talk; where are the gifts?'"

This pastor actually enlisted his sister to teach him how to buy gifts for his wife. In conclusion he said to me, "I now have given my wife a gift every week for thirteen weeks. You wouldn't believe the woman! She is smiling again. I have never seen her this happy. She is giving me words of affirmation. She tells me how good-looking I am and what a good speaker I am. I haven't felt this good in seventeen years."

Do you see what happened? They finally connected. There are thousands of couples like this who are sincere and love each other, but they are not *connecting*. When we choose to understand one another better and then love with the power of the Holy Spirit, we will spend our energy in the way that is most meaningful to our spouse. And the love tank will fill to the top. With emotional warmth surging in the marriage, we can begin to meaningfully address and process our differences and conflicts.

A Short Course on How to Solve an Argument

A true *conflict* happens when the two of you disagree on an issue and you both feel strongly about your positions. If you don't have strong feelings, it's not a conflict; it's just a difference of opinion. So how should we communicate when we have conflicts?

Deal with Anger

Anger is the most common emotion associated with conflict. If we don't deal with it directly, we won't resolve the conflict.

One way to defuse anger is to take a temporary time-out. This idea springs from Proverbs 30:33, which says, "The churning of anger produces strife." In other words, if you keep on talking when you are angry about something, you will likely stir up more trouble.

Ephesians 4:26 warns, "Be angry, and yet do not sin." Notice carefully, it is not a sin to feel angry; but when you do feel angry, don't sin. A time-out can keep you from sinning.

Once the two of you agree on this technique, you can simply use the time-out sign—making a *T* with your hands. This will mean, "Babe, I am about to lose my temper and I don't want to." If your spouse gives you the time-out sign, don't keep talking. One lady told me, "I don't like that time-out stuff. If we have a problem, I want to sit down here and solve it." And I said, "You are likely to sit down there and make it worse."

Don't get me wrong; I am only suggesting a temporary time-out. I'm not talking about three months. I am talking about thirty minutes or an hour, just long enough to let the temperature come down. And during your time-out, each person examines his or her own anger or frustration. You ask yourself questions like, "Why am I angry about this? Is it what my spouse is saying? Is it the *way* it's being said? Is it the way my spouse is looking at me?" Gaining a clearheaded view of the source of the anger can help defuse the anger itself and hasten resolution of the real conflict.

Take Turns Talking

After the time-out, you say to your spouse, "Okay, honey, I think I am under control. I really appreciated the time-out. Is this a good time to talk?" And if it is not a good time to talk, you schedule a better time.

When you do sit down to talk, one of you should take five minutes and share your side without the other person interrupting, then the other spouse gets five minutes to share without interruption. You take as many turns as you like back and forth, but never interrupt each other.

I'm asked sometimes, "Isn't that rather unusual? I have never heard of such a thing—taking turns talking."

Yes, it is very unusual, and that's the problem. Here's what's

typical: "Okay, darling, I think I am under control. I really appreciate the time-out. Is this a good time to talk? What I was trying to say before I got angry was . . ."

And the spouse says, "I know, darling, what I was trying to say was . . ."

"I know that, darling, but . . ."

"I know but . . ."

"Well, that's what gets me right there . . ."

"And that's what gets *me* . . ."

About five rounds of this and somebody loses it, walks out, and slams the door. Communication shuts down and we don't talk about that topic anymore because we're afraid if we talk about that, we will get back into an argument—and we don't like arguments.

We don't have to live like that. We *can* solve our conflicts. We just need to remember that rule from our childhood: Take turns.

Practice Listening

When your spouse is talking, listen. James 1:19 reads, "Let everyone be quick to hear, slow to speak and slow to anger." In context this Scripture is talking about hearing the Word of God. But the principle certainly has an application in human relationships. When your spouse is talking, don't use the time to reload your guns. *Listen.*

Listen to Both Facts and Feelings

You are not likely to resolve a conflict if you don't hear the *feelings.*

A wife says to her husband, "I don't understand it. Three nights this week you came home an hour and a half late. You didn't bother to call me. What was I supposed to do? Two nights I had dinner on the table; the kids were climbing the wall, and no husband. Do you want me to wait an hour and a half on you? If you love me, the least you can do is call me."

What are the *facts*? He came home later than she anticipated three nights this week. Two nights she had dinner on the table. The kids were agitated. One night she didn't know if they were eating in or going out.

But what is she *feeling*? Frustration. Unloved. The typical husband would respond to her facts and ignore her feelings. Most men would say something like, "Now, just a minute. I was not an hour and a half late last night. I looked at my watch when I came in and I was only forty-five minutes late. What do you mean an hour and a half? You always exaggerate. That's what gets me about you."

Do you expect that these two are going to have a tender evening together? If they are to resolve this conflict, they must listen and respond to each other's feelings, not just argue the facts.

Seek to Understand

Put yourself in the shoes of your spouse and understand why he or she might *think* these thoughts and *feel* these feelings.

A spouse needs to understand that this works both ways. In the illustration I just shared, here's what the husband thinks: *I came home late. I didn't call her. But I am a salesman. I am fighting for a $100,000 sale. I'm supposed to say to my customer, "Excuse me, I'm going to be late. I must call my wife." What will that do for sales? Clients will walk right out of my office.*

I am not asking the wife to agree with this husband. I am asking her to try to understand how he might *think* what he is thinking and *feel* what he is feeling. Do you understand his feelings? He is experiencing fear. He is afraid he is going to lose the sale—and possibly his business.

Express Understanding

Let your partner know that you have listened and understood to the best of your ability. In this illustration the husband would say something like this to his wife: "You know, darling, as I listen to you, I think I understand what you are saying. When I don't call, you don't know whether I'll be home when expected or an hour and a half later. You don't know whether to go ahead and feed the children or hang on for ten more minutes. And I guess we hadn't discussed Tuesday night; you didn't know if we were planning to eat in or go out.

"The other thing I hear you saying is when I don't call, you feel like I don't love you. I have to be honest with you; the thought never crossed my mind that you would feel unloved. But, as I hear what you are saying, I can understand how you might feel that way."

The wife responds: "Honey, as I listen to you, I guess I understand what you are saying. If you interrupted your sales presentation to call me, your customer might take that as an opportunity to walk out on you and you would lose the sale."

In this home there will be no fight tonight. Now that they each understand both sides of the conflict, they are prepared to move forward toward a solution.

Seek a Resolution

Once you have defused any anger, listened intently to each other, and expressed understanding, the only remaining question is, "How can we solve this problem?" Two committed adults looking for a solution will together find one.

WE MARRY HUMAN BEINGS

I want to challenge you to agree with one assumption that will help immeasurably in solving your conflicts. If you are married, you are married to a human being. Humans don't all think the same way; they don't all feel the same way. They never will. And you are married to one. So, when we realize we are disagreeing and both feel strongly about it, we should just say, "Wait a minute. I believe we are having one of those conflicts. Let's sit down here and listen. Do you want to go first or do you want me to go first?"

Every time you pull a conflict out from under the rug and resolve it, you grow closer together. By keeping the love tank full and learning how to resolve our conflicts, we have removed two of the biggest barriers to making marriage last for the long haul.

And there will be more than enough *tingles* too.

Dr. Gary Chapman is the director of Marriage and Family Life Consultants, Inc. He has served as a pastor and is a speaker and the author of a number of books. He and his wife, Karolyn, live in North Carolina.

The material presented by Dr. Chapman in this chapter is based primarily on two of his books: The Five Love Languages *(Northfield Publishers, 1995) and* The Other Side of Love: Handling Anger in a Godly Way *(Moody Press, 1999).*

7

Conflict: Sign of a Normal Marriage

GARY AND BARBARA ROSBERG

One fall afternoon Gary was counseling an engaged couple. They had dated for eleven years. (Was there some fear of commitment here?) There they were on his couch, sitting very close to each other. The woman was rubbing her fiancé's neck, and he was nearly drooling. Gary was watching this thinking, *Come on, you guys! Give me a break!* He decided to alter the mood with a question: "How do you two deal with conflict?"

They looked at him and nearly in unison said, "We have never had a conflict!"

"Never had a conflict?" He was incredulous. "And you have been dating all this time?" They talked some more and Gary said, "You're getting married after Thanksgiving, just before Christmas—right?"

"Yes," they responded.

"That means you have just one more national holiday as single adults. I'm just curious: Where are you going to spend Christmas?"

At exactly the same time, they both said, "My parents' house."

They turned to look at each other, and Gary clapped his hands and said, "We've got a conflict!"

It's the truth: Show us any relationship of any time and experience, and we will show you conflict. Conflict is not a problem in marriage; it's as normal as breathing. And what else would we expect out of two such different beings as a man and a woman?

Does This Sound Familiar?

Forgive our understatement when we say women and men are different: different backgrounds, different personalities, different temperaments, and different interests. We often differ in the way we relate to people. All these differences can create conflict. Here's a dialogue between us. See if you identify with any of these differences:

Gary: I love sports.

Barbara: I'm not a sports fan. I love art. And I love slow walks through the woods.

Gary: I don't like slow walks. I want to get my heart rate up, because I have high cholesterol. I like treadmills. And I like to get up at the crack of dawn.

Barbara: I like to sleep until the crack of noon. I love staying up late at night.

Gary: I don't like staying up late at night. I'm toast by about 7:00 P.M. That doesn't give us much time to have conflicts—that's the good news! Another thing—I really like action flicks.

Barbara: Not me, I love sensitive movies. You know there is nothing quite like going with your girlfriends to see a real tearjerker.

Gary: After speaking at a conference, I like to reenergize myself by being around people.

Barbara: I can't wait to be alone in our room to regroup. We even travel differently. I love to see the sights, and if there is an outlet mall within a hundred miles, let's veer off track to see it.

Gary: I just want to get where we're going. I bought a car with an eighty-gallon gas tank. Our family has the record for seeing twelve national memorials in three states in twelve minutes. We stopped, threw the kids out, took a picture, and kept on moving! Oh, and I love a nice hot cup of java.

Barbara: I love a glass of hot green tea with lemon. And I love to tell a story and draw it out a bit.

Gary: And I love to say when she is going on and on, "Barb, quit circling the airport and land that plane!"

Barbara: But, we both love the Lord.

Gary: And we both love our kids.

Barbara: And we both love each other.

Gary: Baby, Baby, Baby!

Barbara: We are so different, but we are so the same too.

Gary: God created us with enough similarities so that we can understand each other and listen to each other.

Barbara: And God created us with enough differences so that we would truly know that we need each other.

Wouldn't life be pretty boring if we were exactly alike?

THE CONFLICT LOOP OPENS

When different types of people like us—and you—mix, there will be conflict. This causes a disruption in the relationship, or an *open loop*.

An open loop always starts with some type of an offense, and it doesn't matter what the offense is. Maybe your mate said something that just made you mad. Or it could be a larger matter like betrayal or being lied to. Maybe the offense is just a series of small things that have combined into a single huge irritation.

Regardless of the offense, when it opens up the loop, it is going to cause an emotional response. Emotions are God-given, and we need to understand and accept them. But when we respond *emotionally* to a hurt and become angry, we often drive away the very person we love the most instead of drawing him or her closer to us.

It's critical to know that a wife and husband in conflict tend to communicate very differently. One of us may tend to withdraw; the other may tend to overcommunicate. As a woman, Barbara likes to communicate a lot. By processing her emotions out loud and listening to them, she is able to formulate answers and make decisions.

"I know sometimes I treat Gary like he is a girlfriend," Barbara says, "because girlfriends volley the communication back and forth like the ball in a good tennis game. In a conflict I'll talk and talk and talk, bringing up many issues. Listening to this, Gary might bog down because he will want to solve each and every one of the issues. But I'm not ready or wanting to solve anything yet because I still need a lot more verbal processing."

Knowing how to listen to wives is a tough thing for husbands. When wives are feeling hurt, their husbands want to jump in and apply bandages. Men were trained to provide for, protect, and take care of their wives. "So," Gary says, "when Barb doesn't let me fix something and just wants me to do 'nothing' but listen, I tend to become angry or to withdraw."

THE TEMPTATION TO ANGER

When guys receive an offense in a conflict, most will scoot right past the emotion of the hurt because those feelings make them feel too vulnerable. They jump to what is called a *secondary emotion*, which most of the time is anger. And poorly handled anger too often ends up wounding the spouse.

Anger in itself is not wrong. The apostle Paul wrote, "Be angry, and yet do not sin; do not let the sun go down on your anger" (Eph. 4:26).

Have you ever gone to bed angry or mad at your mate? We have. You lay your head on the pillow, and though you are upset with your mate, your heart is still in fairly good shape, pliable like wet cement. But by the time you wake up in the morning, your heart can be as hard as concrete.

That's how we sin in our anger. Even if we confront it immediately, it can take us three days or more to blast that hardness out of our hearts. How can we prevent this?

The first thing we encourage you to do is to ask yourself: "Does anger have a hold over me? Does it control me?" If it does, then confess to God that it is harming your relationship. Release the anger and ask God to help you in granting forgiveness. You will not experience true resolution until you empty yourself of the anger, place it at the foot of the cross, and then with the help of the Holy Spirit, turn back actively to appreciating your mate.

THE TEMPTATION TO WITHDRAW

When we marry, the old way of dealing with issues independently as a single adult is supposed to be replaced by marital teamwork. When we face trials like conflict, we are to tackle them together.

But the problem is that the enemy of God does not want you to go through problems *together*. The devil wants to make you an island. His main tool is to deceive you, and a part of that deception is to make you think that only you can take care of your own hurts and problems. He wants to distance you from your mate. He wants you to think your spouse is the enemy. He wants to isolate you. And when you become isolated, your marriage is at risk.

Do you have an *open loop* related to conflict right now in your relationship? You may be thinking, *My spouse has been hard on me.*

You don't know what has happened. There has been adultery. There has been betrayal. There has been disappointment. In spite of how this feels, for *your* good the Lord wants you to move through this hurt and to draw closer to your mate.

For many people the idea of drawing nearer to the person who has caused severe pain seems impossible and not wise. You may protest, "You don't understand what my mate has done!" Or, "I'll just get hurt again."

Think of it this way: Imagine your hands extended in front of you and give your relationship with your mate a value and weight in one hand, and assign a value and weight to the issue that is tormenting you in the other hand. We're confident you will conclude that the value and weight of your relationship is greater than that of the troubling issue. That is the message God is crying out to you in the context of your covenant marriage.

It will take courage to step back toward your mate, to be obedient to Christ, and to resolve it His way. *But before you do anything,* before you approach your mate about the very real issues, you must talk to God and prepare your heart. If you skip this vital stage, you will not go to your mate with the right spirit. If you don't come to your mate in humility, then he or she will be cautious and afraid of what is going to happen next.

These three steps will allow God to prepare your heart:

Pray About the Situation

What is in your heart now really doesn't matter—anger, resentment, insecurity, betrayal, the way your spouse treats the opposite sex. Regardless of the type or severity of the issues, talk about them with God. Be sure to listen to what He says back to you.

Read and Receive the Word

We cannot enjoy transformed lives and truly follow Christ unless we are reading the Word of God and allowing it to mold and purify our character. If you avoid the Word, you can develop a hard heart in fifteen minutes or less on any day of the week.

Write It Down

Write down your thoughts and pleadings to God; those changes you know your mate needs to experience; those heart attitudes in yourself where you need God to make a shift. Record your insights from the Word and God's answers and directions found in prayer.

Once your heart is prepared, then you are ready to take the final steps toward resolution—*closing the loop* of conflict.

CLOSE THE LOOP

This is the good part in confronting conflict. You go to your mate and say, "You are more important than this issue." You begin to communicate. You show that you have renounced the hurt and the anger and refused to embrace resentment and bitterness. You have stepped closer to your mate to say, "I care enough about you and us to risk coming to you. Let's talk about this thing."

You communicate your willingness to allow your mate to talk while you listen—and vice versa. You connect with each other and experience the emotion of walking through the issue as a team.

We call this communication technique *putting a spotlight on your mate*.

That's really what a good listener does. The goal is to understand what the speaker is saying. When that spotlight is on your mate, he or she is the person onstage and you are the audience. Your partner gets to fully express thoughts without any interruptions.

After you have spoken, listened, and connected heart-to-heart, then you are ready to resolve the conflict. This is when you say, "What are we going to do to make the necessary changes?" This begins the restoration of the relationship and moves you to the precious, tender area of forgiveness.

THE NECESSARY STEP OF FORGIVENESS

Regardless of the offense, you must know how important it is to forgive. As great as the step of forgiveness may seem, you will not find freedom without forgiveness.

What is blocking the way for you to forgive? Pride? Resentment? Anger? What are you holding on to? Is there something from the past that has a bigger hold on you than anything your mate has done?

When you release forgiveness over your mate, then God is able to release healing into your heart too.

Here is how you do so:

Take turns going to each other and confessing what you have done to wound each other. Say to your partner, "I am wrong for what I did. And more than that, I am sorry about what I did."

Then you move from "I am wrong and sorry" to *repentance*, which means that you are choosing not to return to the old behavior that so deeply wounded your mate.

Finally, after these steps, you ask the critical question, "Will you forgive me?"

Be aware that trust will have to be rebuilt. For anyone who has experienced a strong sense of betrayal, it may even take a couple of years to reestablish trust in your marriage.

When you are rebuilding trust you need three things:

First, lots of time with one another to replenish that love bank, to deposit tender care back into your marriage. The repentant behavior should include many specific acts that show kindness and caring.

Second, you need to pray together for your marriage and for one another. Also pray individually to keep your heart soft. Daily offenses will happen, and you will need to have a soft heart prepared to talk about them.

Third, guard your marriage. Shore up those boundaries in the relationship so that the enemy of God cannot get a stronghold within the borders of your covenant marriage. Remain vigilant, protecting your marriage from the tendency to get hard-hearted. Be teachable with one another about risks and insecurities in your marriage or where you see your spouse vulnerable to the enemy's ploys.

If you have a hard heart toward your mate now, for the sake of your marriage, your family, and the glory of God, take steps to soften that heart and pull back toward your mate.

Close the loop on conflict. Stay tenderhearted as you learn to love, honor, and cherish each other.

Dr. Gary and Barbara Rosberg, speakers and authors, together host a daily syndicated call-in radio program, America's Family Coaches . . . LIVE! *Gary and Barbara coauthored* The 5 Love Needs of Men and Women *and a HomeBuilders couple's study entitled* Improving Communication in Your Marriage. *Married for more than twenty-five years, they are the parents of two adult daughters. The Rosbergs live in Iowa.*

Kill Those Relationship Germs!

GARY SMALLEY

There are many ways to have a great marriage but basically only four ways to ruin one. I call these four the *relationship germs*, which affect every couple unless they are aware of them and know how to knock them out.

The good news is that there's an inexpensive antibiotic that kills these germs and will bring relational health to your life that you have never known before.

Just to show you how prevalent the germs are and how easily they infect our lives, I want to tell a story of how I managed in a one-hour period to infect my marriage with all four of these bugs.

Several years ago my wife, Norma, and I were in Honolulu,

Hawaii, to lead a seminar. We had arrived a few days early to enjoy some downtime with our seminar staff. On a Monday morning I woke up at 6:00 A.M. and was staring at the ceiling. Norma was still asleep and I was thinking, *I don't want to stay here much longer, so I am going to get up.*

So I went out, and the scene was breathtaking! There was some predawn light, but the sun hadn't yet risen over Diamond Head. Honolulu Bay reflected the city lights. No wind—it was absolutely beautiful!

I am a spontaneous person, so I thought, *Ooh, wouldn't this be a great place to work on our marriage goals? I can wake up Norma, my best friend, and we can come out here on the balcony and talk about what we want to accomplish in our relationship in the next year—maybe even order some coffee or something!*

It seemed like such a great idea. I sneaked back into the still-dark bedroom and put my face right up next to hers and tapped her. She woke with a start. "What?" she said.

"Hey, I have a great idea! You won't believe how beautiful it is out on the balcony. The sun is not up yet. We could share this experience and work on our marriage goals. What do you think?"

"What time is it?" she asked.

"Six o'clock."

"I told you last night that we're on vacation and that I wanted to sleep until seven o'clock," she said. "Go out there and have a ball, and I will join you at seven."

"You're already awake!" I answered. "Come on out now—you're going to miss the sunrise!"

"And I'm going to *stay* awake unless you get out of here and let me go back to sleep!"

"Come on!" I said. I grabbed the covers and pulled them off a little way. She pulled them back up! I was thinking, *This is my best friend, and I'm stronger than she is!* So I yanked the covers completely off, grabbed her by the ankles, and started pulling her out of bed. This was really fun!

Then she said something that hurt my feelings. It shocked me, and I thought, *Where did that come from?* And so I got real defensive and shot a zinger back at her. After that, we had an hour's discussion while she stayed in bed. It wasn't about our marriage goals. We brought up the entire history of our life together, and almost every mean thing we could say to each other came out of our mouths.

After this hour of going back and forth and being combative, Norma said, "I can't believe we started our day like this. I don't want to talk to you anymore. I'm going to go to breakfast." So, she got dressed, and as she left I heard her mumble, "I hope you are not following me!"

This was Monday, and in four more days I would be doing my weekend marriage seminar. I think you will understand why I don't feel good about doing my marriage seminar with my wife not speaking to me! So, since I'm supposed to be an expert on damaged relationships, I knew I had do some quick repair work on my own.

During the day, I tested the waters with Norma. We were in the hotel lobby around noon, and I furtively took her hand to see how things were progressing. She slung it down, and I looked around quickly to see if anybody registering for our seminar had seen this. I was ready to say, "Really! It'll be okay by Friday. Trust me! We fix these damaged things pretty fast."

That night one of our staff couples got engaged. They came back to the hotel about ten o'clock and were very excited. So our group, including Norma, walked next door to have a little celebration at an ice cream parlor.

When we got into the store, we yelled, "Hey, this couple just got engaged!" It was packed with people and everyone clapped. We ate our ice cream and I was about to pay the bill. I tried to give the manager the money but she ignored me. Then she leaned across the counter and said to the engaged couple, "I don't know you, but I have some marriage advice for you." Everybody in the place stopped talking. A profound moment. She said, "There is this guy on television, and I think his name is Gary Smalley. He has these videos, and we ordered them and they have really helped our marriage."

Our staff looked at me, assuming I had set this up. "I had nothing to do with this," I said.

So someone said to the manager, "That's Gary Smalley trying to pay you!" She screamed, ran around the counter, and gave me a big hug. It was such an embarrassing scene!

As we started to leave, Norma walked over to me, put her arm around me, and whispered in my ear, "You ought to order those videos!" Then she smiled because by this time we were once again getting along.

But that's how the germs can infect any marriage. I want to tell you about how they work and how to wipe them out.

The Four Germs

Germ 1: Withdrawal from an Argument

Your partner has hurt your feelings and, with emotions boiling, you are afraid the spat is going to get out of control. So it seems better to just vanish, to drop the whole issue and escape the conflict. This kind of withdrawal is not to be confused with choosing to take a time-out or a breather to cool off. This germ is rather an avoidance of the conflict altogether.

Germ 2: Escalation During an Argument

You escalate the scope and stakes in a disagreement because your competitive instincts take over. You want to win your point, so you pump more fuel onto the fire. Soon this germ spreads from the issue at hand and makes your whole relationship sick.

Germ 3: Belittling Your Mate

This may be the number one killer of marriages in America. This germ flourishes whenever you think, *I am so superior to my mate!* We all know how destructive such an attitude is.

For years Dr. John Gottman has done research with couples in his "Seattle Love Lab" to determine scientifically just what makes a marriage endure or fail. He has identified four types of negativity that he believes are lethal to a marriage, of which *contempt* is the worst. Gottman has found that the negative vibes associated with contempt affect a person's health. He says that those couples "are more likely to suffer from infectious illnesses (colds, flu, and so on) than other people."[1]

Germ 4: Dwelling on a Mate's Negative Qualities

If you concentrate on negative things, guess what happens? You will start seeing negative qualities in your spouse even if they aren't there. No doubt because of the basic sinful bent of human beings, we find it a lot easier to see the negative than the positive in other people.

We know that hosting any of these four germs is not God's will. He asks that we live "in peace with one another" (1 Thess. 5:13) and "regard one another as more important than [ourselves]" (Phil. 2:3). That should be our goal—harmony, humility, and unity in our marriage.

THE GERM-KILLING ANTIBIOTIC

Here is the tremendous wonder drug for annihilating these four germs: It is called honor. I am going to give you the three required *doses* of this antibiotic. The wonderful thing is that this drug has no harmful side effects and it's impossible to overdose on it!

Dose 1: Decide Your Mate Is Highly Valuable

Even though men and women are very different, let's choose to thank God for this and blend our strengths to be a strong team. The husband must decide to value his wife's personality, uniqueness, background, interests, opinions, concerns, expectations, and so on. The wife must do the same with her husband. It does not matter that each of them thinks differently, likes different things, and processes emotions differently.

Aren't we all special creations of God? If you can see your mate's smile as God's signature on his or her life, then every time you look at that person, you will think, *Oh, unbelievable! I am actually living with a person who is autographed by God. Unreal! That's amazing!* You will want to say to your mate, "Oh, just to be in the same room with you is so exciting!" Some morning when you wake up, jump out of bed and give your spouse a standing ovation! Practice outdoing each other in giving honor to such a valuable person.

Dose 2: List the Positive Qualities of Your Mate

Write down all the things you appreciate, adore, or find wonderful in your spouse. Only include the positive nothing negative. This dose is so powerful it can just about knock out all the relationship germs on its own.

The reason this is so potent is that if you force yourself to find something positive on a daily basis, the more you look the more you will see.

One researcher in our country performed several experiments with more than one hundred couples that were really strained and heading toward divorce. One of the tests was for each couple to go home, write positive lists about their mates, and then share them with each other without discussing any negatives. After doing this, a significant majority of those couples had an improved marriage and stayed together. That's incredible! All they did was this one thing—developed a grateful heart toward their mate by listing the good things they saw in them.

I have more than four single-spaced sheets of positive things about Norma. When our relationship is strained, I sometimes pull the list up on my computer and start reading. It isn't five minutes before I am warm again toward her. It changes my affections and feelings that rapidly.

I now realize that this is one application of the Scripture verse that says, "Whatever is honorable . . . let your mind dwell on these things" (Phil. 4:8). That is exactly what we can do in marriage.

Dose 3: Tell the Positive Things Regularly
You should do this verbally, but don't forget the little sticky notes, cards, billboards! Honor your mate in front of your kids by telling your children how thrilled you are with their mommy or daddy. Let them go back to your mate and tell them what Dad or Mom said. Tell your friends about your mate. Tell your church about your mate. Sing praises from the housetop about how wonderful your mate is.

Norma and I know all about the germs. We argued about so many things for so many years and never understood the nature of these relational bacteria. We finally got it. We realized the greatest thing we could do in life was to honor one another.

And we're still at it. You name it; we differ. That's okay because we seek a win-win solution to everything. This year we are concentrating on twelve major areas where we must find a win-win. It will probably take six months, but it's worth it. When we are done we will be thrilled with the results.

Honoring your spouse destroys the germs. Why not put this antibiotic to work in clearing any disease out of your covenant marriage?

Dr. Gary Smalley is one of America's best-known experts on family relationships. He has authored and coauthored a number of best-selling books, including The Blessing and For Better or For Worse. His seminar, "Marriage for a Lifetime," has been attended by thousands of couples. Gary and his wife, Norma, have been married thirty-six years and now work with their sons, Greg and Michael, in ministry. The schedule of Smalley seminars is available on the Internet at www.smalleyonline.com.

PART 4

"To have and to hold . . ."

9

God Loves Sex

DAN ALLENDER

I don't remember too much of my wedding day. We were to marry at seven o'clock in the evening, which was a ridiculous mistake. The hours dragged. I sat catatonically the whole day awaiting the event. I was out of it during the ceremony, feeling like I was in a dimly lit room. Somehow, I ended up standing in front of the pastor. Words were being said. And I was thinking, *How did I get here?*

The reverend came to that section that says, "to have and to hold," and something in me brightened. In our relationship there had been no touch between the two of us, no kissing or holding. But I knew what was coming now would be good. Our extended fast, denying intimacy, was about to end. Let the feast begin! So I said, "to have and to hold," and came alive.

The ceremony ended, and we made our way to the reception, which lasted forever—at least that's what it felt like. I don't know why we didn't do a drive-through reception; just rent a fast-food restaurant and have people drive up, give you the gift, take a sack of cake, say hello and good-bye, and drive on. We could have finished in thirty minutes!

The reception finally ended, but then we observed the tradition that you don't go out into the world in the same clothes you wore for the wedding. It seemed like it took another hour or two for my new wife to change. Finally, we left.

We arrived at our honeymoon chamber. At last we would move into that intimate moment that I had prepared for with my heart, body, and soul. I knew not to rush things. I had brought some bath gel and a candle or two. As soon as we walked in the door, I figured my wife would take a bath, I would prepare, and then *love* would begin. Instead, when we got through the door, my wife came to me and opened her arms wide. I thought, *This is it!* She put her hands on my shoulders and said, "I'm hungry. What do you think about ordering a pizza?"

At that moment I realized I could crumble on the ground and start kicking my legs and my arms and have a fit or I could "pull rank" and demand sex. Neither seemed an appropriate male response. It dawned on me then that to have a sexual relationship with my spouse I needed not just to wait on my wife and the pizza deliveryman, but I also needed to wait on God to know the best moment for us to join together.

This understanding is the basis for my first key conclusion: *To truly love another, you must first have a relationship with God.*

You must wait on the Lord to receive the desires of your heart. And you must know that satisfying sex will never survive the heat of selfishness—your own demands, your pressure on your spouse, or your backing away from your spouse.

If we function as a servant, we find that our sexuality not only will bring pleasure and intimacy, but also profound joy. From the beginning this is what God had in mind.

It may surprise us but it's true: God *loves* sex. He designed it, He made it, and He rejoices in it. But, as always, whatever God loves, evil hates. And evil seeks to create in our world—through immorality, adultery, advertising, the Internet—an image of sex that is misleading or false.

We also know that evil works to make our own sexual relationship with our spouse feel demanding or awkward. A suprisingly large percentage of married people fail to talk to each other about their sexuality. Why? Because although we often think about sex, talk about sex, and claim to enjoy sex, many married people have learned to live with little sex. And they live with that little bit in a way in which their sexuality, even if they feel it is adequate, becomes dry and boring.

How much God loves sex is revealed explicitly in the Song of Solomon. In this erotic love poetry tucked away in the Old Testament, we find Solomon saying this about his wife:

> How beautiful are your feet in sandals,
> O prince's daughter!
> The curves of your hips are like jewels,
> The work of the hands of an artist.

Your navel is like a round goblet
Which never lacks mixed wine;
Your belly is like a heap of wheat
Fenced about with lilies. (Song 7:1–2)

Hmmm. What does this mean? If I told my wife that I really liked her navel, I don't think it would excite her. And if I said to her, "Your belly is, ah, sort of like, I don't know, a paddock," that would be wacky! The truth is that with this poetic language you need to use your imagination. The word *navel* doesn't literally mean belly button. And the writer is not referring to the area where you buckle your belt when he says the belly is like a heap of wheat. He is talking figuratively about the beauty of a woman's private anatomy.

Solomon continues:

> Your two breasts are like two fawns,
>
> Twins of a gazelle.
>
> Your neck is like a tower of ivory,
>
> Your eyes like the pools in Heshbon
>
> By the gate of Bath-rabbim;
>
> Your nose is like the tower of Lebanon,
>
> Which faces toward Damascus. (7:3–4)

This also needs to be culturally interpreted. I don't recommend you say to your wife, "You know, your nose looks like the Tower of Pisa!"

Solomon goes on:

> Your head crowns you like Carmel,
>
> And the flowing locks of your head are like purple threads . . .
>
> How beautiful and how delightful you are,
>
> My love, with all your charms! (7:5–6)

Now, if that does not show a God who loves sex, I don't know how to convince you.

But it's not just men who feel aroused by the sight of their spouse. In Song of Solomon, chapter 5, the woman gets her turn and speaks:

> My beloved is dazzling and ruddy,
>
> Outstanding among ten thousand.
>
> His head is like gold, pure gold;
>
> His locks are like clusters of dates,

And black as a raven.
His eyes are like doves,
Beside streams of water,
Bathed in milk,
And reposed in their setting.
His cheeks are like a bed of balsam,
Banks of sweet-scented herbs;
His lips are lilies,
Dripping with liquid myrrh.
His hands are rods of gold
Set with beryl;
His abdomen is carved ivory
Inlaid with sapphires.
His legs are pillars of alabaster
Set on pedestals of pure gold;
His appearance is like Lebanon,
Choice as the cedars.
His mouth is full of sweetness.
And he is wholly desirable.
This is my beloved and this is my friend,
O daughters of Jerusalem. (Song 5:10–16)

Again, this woman is using figurative language to describe beautifully every part of her naked lover's body. She sees it all and adores it.

These erotic words underscore one core thing about sexual relationship: Foreplay begins in verbal confession about the loveliness of your lover's body.

God is not ashamed of sex. In fact, He seems very pleased with this brilliant part of His creation.

SEX AS GOD PLANNED

Our sexuality is the most fragile part of our relationship with our spouse. In many ways it is like a Stradivarius violin, a very expensive, exquisite instrument that is affected by temperature and humidity. If the instrument is poorly treated, it will play out of tune. The violin will still produce some sounds, but it will not be the music that its creator intended. Sex plays like a mint Stradivarius in a covenantal relationship where we know God and experience the freedom to follow His plan. To make music sexually, we must understand God's plan, which includes the reality of how God has made us.

Before sin came into the world, the Bible says that Adam and Eve were naked but knew no shame. Clearly, as a result of the Fall, we live in a world where there will be some fear, awkwardness, and inhibition, even during moments with your spouse. But often we don't want to think or talk about our sexual experience. It is amazing how people can spend thousands of dollars learning to do a skill like golf more effectively and yet literally not spend one dollar on a book, a seminar, or a tape series on a core area of life like sexuality.

Now, the question we have to answer to our own satisfaction is, who designed this? How has God made us sexually? It is either madness or it is a miracle, and the answer will determine the quality of your sexual relationship.

A part of the answer is that He has rigged our bodies so that we cannot know real pleasure, real intimacy, and real joy without having a heart to know Him and to surrender to our mate. If you hate your husband's body because his body responds so differently, you are not just hating a man but also criticizing God's creativity. If you hate your wife's body because she seems to take forever to arouse, you're not just frustrated with a frigid female; you are disputing God's ability as Creator.

The truth is that you cannot love a man without serving his body. And you cannot love a woman without serving her body. You must have a core commitment to God to accept how He has made us and called us to express our sexuality in the marriage relationship.

So is this madness or miracle? I believe the miracle is this: We cannot enjoy ourselves or our spouse unless we bless the way God has made not only us, but also our mate. If you do not bless God over your lover's body, then you will not appreciate and embrace the way he or she has been made.

That brings me to a second conclusion: *You must have a relationship with God to sustain the heartache, the waiting, and the struggles that come in all sexual relationships.* If you don't know the kindness of

God, if you do not know the strength of God to endure some of the shame, hurt, and heartache, then you will not be free to be able to give to your spouse the way God intends.

EMOTIONAL INTIMACY PRECEDES PHYSICAL INTIMACY

You have heard the old saying "Sex doesn't begin in the bedroom . . . it begins in the kitchen." Through a personal story—a type of sex-in-the-kitchen illustration—I can explain why.

I once asked my wife before leaving to speak at an "I Still Do" conference, "Do you recall any one sexual moment in our lives?" I definitely had a particular incident in my mind.

She said, "Let me think about it . . . I think it was the time we came back from dropping the kids off . . ."

"Eagle Lake, right?" I interrupted.

"Right. How did you know?"

To be honest, the day we both recalled had been one where I would have predicted, "Anything but good sex will come of this."

On that improbable afternoon we were driving our kids to a wonderful Christian camp at Eagle Lake. It was a gorgeous Colorado summer day, blue sky, the wind cool but the air still warm. We had our sunroof open and the wind was blowing through. Our two daughters and our son were in the backseat with a young puppy. As we moved down the highway, we sang, we talked, and we laughed.

Nearing the camp and beginning to wind up some mountain roads, my son looked at me via the rearview mirror and said, "Dad . . . I'm not feeling well."

"Andrew, we are only about twenty minutes from the camp," I said. "We'll be there really soon. Just relax your body. We'll get you there. I know you are a little carsick, but just hold on."

About thirty seconds later, I heard the first sounds—the movement of whatever was in him began. As he regurgitated, the girls in the backseat screamed. My wife heard and saw what was happening and shouted to me, "Stop, stop!"

In my mind I was laying out a strategy: Ahead about three blocks I saw a health club. I was thinking, *If we stop here on the side of the road and get Andrew out, maybe he'll throw up some more outside the car. But after 80 percent is already in, what difference does another 15–20 percent make? If we can just get to that health club, there will be water and towels.* So I had a plan. I'm the man. I'm focused. I'm moving.

My mate didn't know or understand my plan, and I did not have time to explain. So she grabbed me and said, "Don't you hear what's happening?"

Finally I drove up to the club and stopped. The kids practically leaped out of the windows. The dog in the backseat was ecstatic with his good fortune. Nobody wanted to clean up the car. Everybody fled about two hundred yards, so I got the privilege of cleaning up the mess *and* holding the dog to make sure it wouldn't run away.

Now, if you had told me this was the prelude to incredible sex about seven hours later, I would have said you were mad. What I failed to anticipate was how my wife would appreciate my taking the responsibility and the servanthood I demonstrated in dealing with Andrew's discomfort and a very messy car. But that, indeed, is the miracle: Sex doesn't begin in the bedroom. If you are willing to learn, then you will know that sex begins in the early part of the day—in the way you speak, the way you touch, the way you are committed, the way you care, the way you serve, the way you grow one another. Grasp the simple concept of how sex begins, and your sexual life will grow beyond all comprehension.

That brings me to a final conclusion: *You must have a will ingness to open the door, not just to spiritual realities that make you more of a servant to the other, but to greater emotional intimacy.* Unfortunately, three enemies crouch along everyone's path to the enjoyment of a growing, enjoyable sexual intimacy.

The first enemy is fear. A sign of this may be the fact that after twenty or thirty years of marriage spouses are still afraid to talk to each other about their sexuality. They cannot put in words what they desire. I have discovered that such fear is often caused by a lack of information. For example, are you aware that only about 65 percent of women are able to have an orgasm during intercourse? Many men and women assume that the total is more like 99 percent—everybody but themselves. If you don't have accurate information, there can be a weight of fear and guilt that you are inadequate sexually.

Another piece of misinformation concerns the number of orgasms a typical woman has. Generally speaking, a woman has an orgasm one out of every four times that she makes love to her husband. So if her husband pressures her to have more orgasms than that, he violates the delicate nature of how God has crafted a woman's body.

The second killer of intimacy is anger. This involves common sense. How could emotional closeness be possible when feelings are raw? Much of the anger related to sex comes from a sense of being misused or misunderstood.

The third killer is disgust. This involves the sense that there is something wrong with my body or something repulsive or wrong with my spouse's body. Either way, closeness at the depth we desire is not going to occur.

These three great killers must be disarmed or you will struggle sexually—as many couples do. But you can continue to move toward each other in hope, knowing that the quest for deeper intimacy lasts a lifetime.

Don't expect after reading this chapter and accepting my three conclusions that your sexual experience suddenly will be fabulous. Start by talking honestly and tenderly. Agree together, "We want a more intimate, satisfying sexual relationship. We want that because it pleases not only us but also the God of the universe and the Lord of our lives."

Sex is holy and earthly, pleasurable and wonderful—transcendent beyond what words can describe. If that is not what you want, you have settled for too little.

Reach out to each other to understand the mystery of this

holy interaction. Draw your hearts together. Underscore the commitment to each other. Open the door to incredible intimacy. God will love it!

Dr. Dan Allender is professor of counseling at Western Seminary in Seattle. He is the author of The Wounded Heart, The Healing Path, *and other books. Dr. Allender and his wife, Rebecca, have three children.*

3-D Sex

TIM AND DARCY KIMMEL

When it comes to sexual satisfaction, a lot of people say, "I don't think I can ever experience the kind of sexual intimacy that I hoped for when I got married. It just doesn't seem to click in my relationship with my spouse." We want to prove you wrong. You do have the potential. You might be surprised where you'll find it.

William Randolph Hearst was a very wealthy man. When he started accumulating his vast fortune, he sent his buyers off to Europe to purchase exquisite pieces of art and sculpture. There was one painting in particular that he always wanted. Each time he sent his buyers back out he'd remind them to find and purchase this masterpiece. And each time they would come back with the same discouraging report. "Sorry, Mr. Hearst, we couldn't find it."

Finally, just before Hearst died, one of his buyers came back from a buying trip and announced the news he had always wanted to hear: "We found your painting."

Hearst wanted to know where. "Was it in Switzerland? Italy? Did you find it in the Far East?"

"No," the man answered, "we found it in your warehouse. You owned it all along."

That's what God wants you to know concerning sexual intimacy too. You already have what you need to experience joy and satisfaction in this area. Sadly, for so many couples, sex does not bring joy. What a shame. It doesn't have to be this way. We believe God wants the best for your intimate life. And the good news is, you've had what it takes all along.

Why Sex?

We have been married for almost twenty-eight years, but early on we were pretty naive about this issue of intimacy. Actually, being naive is not the worst place to start in a marriage. Because what we have learned about this topic, we have learned together.

The Kimmels are probably just like you. We live at a hectic pace, so is it any wonder that the intimate side of our marriage gets what is left over in our time and energy? But God wants us to enjoy maximum oneness and ultimate joy in our sexual lives. In order to enjoy this type of intimacy, we must not only blend our bodies but our hearts and souls as well.

The Bible outlines four primary reasons why God gave us this gift of sex within the covenant of marriage.

First of all, sex is for creating life. In Genesis 1:28, God says, "Be fruitful and multiply, and fill the earth." This may be the only commandment that God gave the human race that we have consistently obeyed!

God also gave us the gift of sex as an illustration of oneness. Genesis 2:24 says, "For this cause a man shall leave his father and his mother, and shall cleave to his wife; and they shall become one flesh." This concept of oneness is unparalleled, where two individuals become so intimately acquainted with each other, so bonded, so intertwined in body, soul, and spirit that God sees them as one instead of two. And through love-making God wanted a man and a woman to have a visual illustration of all He desires for us spiritually—a union of our souls with the living God.

God also gave us sex within marriage as a defense against temptation. First Corinthians 7:2, 5 says, "But because of immoralities, let each man have his own wife, and let each woman have her own husband . . . Stop depriving one another, except by agreement for a time that you may devote yourselves to prayer, and come together again lest Satan tempt you because of your lack of self-control." God created us as sexual beings, but He only intends for us to fulfill that need within marriage.

And finally, God gave us this gift of sex for pleasure. It may surprise you that in the Scriptures the purpose of sexual pleasure in marriage is mentioned even more than the purpose of becoming one or being fruitful. Proverbs 5:15, 18–19 provides scriptural encouragement about the priority of pleasure in sex:

> Drink water from your own cistern,
> And fresh water from your own well . . .
> Let your fountain be blessed,
> And rejoice in the wife of your youth.
> As a loving hind and a graceful doe,
> Let her breasts satisfy you at all times;
> Be exhilarated always with her love.

DISCOVERING 3-D SEX

Most people only experience sex at one dimension at most. But the Bible talks about three: *spiritual intimacy*, which is the covenant with each other before God; *emotional intimacy*, which secures our friendship as couples; and *physical intimacy*, which enables us to experience deeper and freer passion as lovers. That's three-dimensional sex. It is not reserved for the rich and the beautiful. Great sex isn't about great looks and muscular bodies.

You look at the slender woman wearing the long white dress in your wedding picture. Maybe now she is pushing a baby buggy and not quite so trim. After having a baby inside you for nine months, skipping rope with an umbilical cord, the truth is that internal wear and tear puts some miles on a body. But when we see that woman, we know that she gave a human being life. That is a beautiful woman!

The guy standing there in your wedding picture might have been well-built. But the guy rolling out of bed in the morning is anything but well-built. But you know what? He loves God, and he prays for his family. He gets up in the morning and goes off to work with a good attitude; he works hard and draws an honest paycheck; he tries to spend his pay well; he loves his kids. He spends time with his wife, he loves her with all of his heart, but his body is showing the ravages of age. To us, that body is a fine vessel.

God wants you to know that your body does not have to look like some hunk or babe from *Bay Watch* to experience 3-D sex.

Spiritual Intimacy

So what is spiritual intimacy in a marriage?

When Adam and Eve were created, they were naked but were not self-conscious. They were transparent at the emotional level, but didn't feel vulnerable. Then sin entered the world. Immediately they sensed their vulnerability and they didn't like it. Impulse drove them to gather fig leaves and make some clothes so they could hide their nakedness. That's the bad news.

Here's the good news. It's a fascinating truth about sex in marriage. We can't go back to the conditions we had with God before the Fall. Sin has locked us out of the Garden forever. But God gives us a taste of Eden through sex. He allows us to experience that sense of being naked and unashamed with our spouse once again.

But there are some things that can keep us from enjoying that Edenic intimacy. Our lives are tainted by sin. Maybe there are past sexual sins; maybe you have had unclean thoughts. Maybe you have some relational and marital regrets and they cause you to want to cover yourself and hide from each other when it comes to sexual intimacy.

How do you cover yourself? Maybe with a busy lifestyle; maybe with excuses; maybe just indifference. Or maybe you hide behind layers of anger that set you up for rejection. Maybe you came from a rigid home life or a leaderless home. Maybe someone took horrible advantage of you.

We want you to know something important: God wants to ease your burden and give you hope. Just as God killed a lamb and took its hide to cover Adam and Eve, the heavenly Father killed the Lamb of God to cover your sins, to forgive you. No matter what is keeping you from experiencing this transparency spiritually, God wants to set you free.

How can we maximize this spiritual intimacy?

One of the things we do to remain spiritually responsive to each other is to pray for one another. And when a man and a woman give themselves totally to each other, it is in their best interest to pray for that investment. Prayer is what keeps our hearts tender and responsive to each other.

Another way to draw close to each other spiritually is to recognize that your mate is a handpicked gift from God and to treat him or her that way.

EMOTIONAL INTIMACY

The second dimension of 3-D sex is emotional intimacy, which is the blending of our hearts. This is the friendship factor, the companionship aspect of a marriage relationship. We may not realize this, but a healthy emotional bond determines how close you can come to experiencing ultimate joy in your sexual experience.

Because of our marriage covenant, we have a safe harbor for our emotions. We can remove our masks and be known and loved by someone unconditionally. As soul mates we can laugh and cry together. Those tears of joy and sorrow bind us together.

However, a number of issues can destroy emotional oneness. Maybe you were brought up in a home where people trafficked in guilt. Maybe there was a ton of anger, or you were told to hold back your emotions and not let them out. Or maybe sex was considered dirty, and you were never allowed to talk about it. Perhaps you lived in a house full of pornography. You ended up with the feeling that there was something flawed about sex. Therefore, you are embarrassed. You can't open up. You're not free to let go. Or maybe you just married somebody who was anticipating a lot more excitement from you and he or she feels cheated. Maybe you started out with the wrong information. Maybe your heart was broken when you were young. Maybe you had premarital sex or an abortion. Maybe you have been through extramarital affairs. Was there a divorce? All these things can block and scar you emotionally.

Don't despair! There's hope. God loves you. He is a God of the second chance. God is a God of a clean slate. He wants to forgive you completely. He took that pain and that shame upon Himself, and He doesn't want you being held back in this area because of what may have happened in the past.

Physical Intimacy

What do we have in the physical intimacy of the blending of our bodies?

First of all, we have God's design. Genesis 1:27 says, "And God created man in His own image, in the image of God He created him; male and female He created them." God created the male and female, two bodies to come together in sexual intercourse. Our ability to give and receive pleasure is no accident; it is a deliberate act of creation.

We also have God's intent. Genesis 1:28 goes on to say that God blessed them and said to them, "Be fruitful and multiply." From the beginning of this first marriage, it was God's intent that a husband and wife would come together and be fruitful. And that is still God's intent for marriage.

Finally, we have God's blessing. Not only did God conclude the creation of the man and woman and their union by declaring it good, but the Scripture has included some enthusiastic endorsement of the sexual union.

In the Song of Solomon we find Solomon and his Shulammite wife engaged in sensual lovemaking. That this appears unashamedly as part of His Word reveals God's blessing on sexual expression in marriage. Solomon's statement— "Eat, Friends; . . . and imbibe deeply, O lovers" (Song 5:1)— could certainly be the very words of God Himself. So when it comes to the blending of our bodies, we have God's enthusiastic endorsement.

OBSTACLES TO 3-D SEX

So with all of that going for us, what keeps us from enjoying each other physically? The biggest obstacle probably is that we are so radically different. Not only are we different as individuals, we are also different as men and women.

We can solve a lot of the conflict that comes from these differences if we can see the sexual act at three different levels, each meeting legitimate needs and purposes. The metaphor of food helps illustrate: First, we have fast-food sex. That is when you don't have a lot of time but you want to meet the need of your spouse. Next, there is home-cooked sex. It is the stick-to-your-ribs type of sex—more fulfilling, more satisfying because you have more time to meet each other's needs on a regular basis. Finally, there is the candlelight dinner sex. These are those special occasions when you set aside an evening or an entire weekend for pleasing each other in a secure, undisturbed place where kids won't walk in with tummy-aches and the telephone solicitors can't find you. These require some extra investment of planning, time, and money.

Here's the challenge. All these levels are necessary to a mutually fulfilling sex life. But having sex at only one of those levels is going to cause a problem. If you have only fast-food sex, you will feel undernourished. If you have only home-cooked sex, it can get dull. If you have only candlelight sex, you'll go broke. So you need all three.

Another obstacle we contend with is that we are two very different people, hardwired differently when it comes to responding to sex. Here's a little closing dialogue on just how different men and women are—and what to do about it to enjoy dynamite 3-D sex.

HOW MEN AND WOMEN RESPOND TO SEX

Darcy: Men can compartmentalize their need for sex. They are able to focus in on it no matter what else is going on. Their interest in sex is like a computer screen saver; it's on all the time. For men, it is their highest priority most of the time.

Tim: Women are much more relational, so sex has to fit into a context. And there are a lot of other priorities that are higher for them, like housekeeping. Some guy might say, "Hey, honey, you want to have sex?" His wife answers, "No, I've got to finish these shirts here, and then I'm going to fold clothes, and then I need to alphabetize my spice rack, and then I have to rearrange the sock drawer. You know, I am a busy woman."

Darcy: Men are much more *body* centered, and that is why it behooves us ladies to care for our bodies and keep them healthy. Men are turned on by sight, fragrance, and tender actions.

Tim: When it comes to being turned on, women are much more *person* centered. They respond to touch, kindness, sensitivity, and to sacrificial actions. In fact, men, I can guarantee that your wife will be far more interested in you physically if when you came home from work instead of plopping in front of the sports channel, you roll up your sleeves and figure out what needs to be done around the house. Fix something, cook something, find something, fold something . . . *do* something!

Darcy: Men like to be physically needed. Has your husband ever said to you, "You know, honey, if I never suggested it, would we ever have sex? Just once, I would like for this to be your idea." I daresay, though, if we had the idea to have sex as often as they did, men would be wearing garlic around their necks!

Tim: One of the greatest sexual needs of women is for security and emotional closeness. There is not a woman alive who doesn't want to sit in the shrine of her husband's heart. Another thing women need when it comes to sex is time— huge chunks of time. So when a guy says something like, "Hey, honey, do you want to have sex?"

"Now?" she asks.

"Yeah."

"We're getting ready to go out."

"So?"

"Our friends are waiting in the living room."

"Yeah, but we said we would be out in five minutes."

(She looks at her watch) "All right! Ready? Set? Go!"

That is not the way women were designed to respond.

Darcy: Men can respond in any context, any place, any time. They are very quick to excite and almost impossible to distract.

Tim: Women, on the other hand, are very easy to distract because they always have this bigger picture in life. God has given them a spy satellite; they are monitoring a lot of things.

You may be sleeping with your wife when suddenly she sits up in bed, stares at the ceiling for a moment, then lies back down and goes back to sleep. Check the paper the next morning; I'll bet the space shuttle went over the house. In sexual activity, women warm up slowly and are very easily distracted.

Then, we have the *big climax*, that very interesting *O* word. When it comes to orgasm, men are faster, more intense. It takes the average man 2.3 minutes to reach orgasm; the average woman, 13 minutes. Wow, I could read the Phoenix telephone directory in 13 minutes!

Darcy: Tim, that's always an option!

SO, HOW DO YOU KEEP ROMANCE ALIVE?

Remember when you were dating and enjoying fun activities together? Be just as creative with sex. Reclaim your bedroom for sex. Take the ironing board down. Relocate that pile of clothes in the corner that has its own area code. Get out of the same routine. Keep passion a priority by planning. Plan a weekend away. If you can't afford this, trade kids with friends so you can be at home without interruptions. The next weekend it can be your friends' turn.

Some husbands need to enroll in a twelve-step program to release the iron grip on the remote control. And it is a new millennium; go out and buy some new underwear!

If you are a wife, you don't need anyone's permission to be sensual. Take care of your body. Use some of that perfume you have been saving for a special time. Clean out your lingerie drawer. If the elastic doesn't snap back, throw those things out. Then encourage your husband to go out and buy you a new nightgown every once in a while.

We agree on this, but Tim asks, "Do other guys get as embarrassed in those lace emporiums in the mall as I do? Here's what always happens to me.

"I go to the mall and hang out in the bookstore across the courtyard from the lingerie store. Once I'm sure none of the kids from the Sunday school class I teach are walking down the mall, I pull a ski mask over my face and walk into the store. Invariably, some young girl waits on me.

"'I'm looking for a nightgown for my wife,' I say. The clerk, beaming, holds some satin thing up next to her.

"'Don't hold it up to you!' I scream.

"Then she holds it up to me.

"'No, no! Don't hold it up to me. Could you just throw it in a heap on the floor? Let me look at it that way.'

"Like most men, that's where I'm hoping it spends the bulk of the evening!"

Dr. Tim and Darcy Kimmel live in Arizona and are the parents of four children. Tim's books include Little House on the Freeway, Raising Kids Who Turn Out Right, Basic Training for a Few Good Men, How to Deal with Powerful Personalities, Homegrown Heroes, *and* Surviving Life in the Fast Lane. *Tim is the president of Family Matters, whose goal is to encourage and equip families to bring out the best in one another and enhance the quality of their culture by living a relevant, biblical lifestyle. For more information go to www.timkimmel.com.*

PART 5

"'Til death
do us part"

Marriage for
the Glory of God!

BOB LEPINE

Right before my twentieth birthday, I came home from college for Christmas break. The first night I was back, I was in the living room and my mom came and sat down on the sofa beside me.

She took a deep breath and said, "I've decided I'm going to leave your dad."

My parents' marriage had not been without problems. Most of the issues in their relationship were compounded by the fact that my dad was an alcoholic and manic-depressive. He had those cycles of highs and lows that made his personality erratic and his behavior difficult. Mom had lived with that for more than fifteen years.

But even though my mom's words should not have been such a surprise, I was stunned. I thought for a moment, and then not able to do anything else, I started to sob. This was odd for me; except for choking up at a tender moment in a movie, I don't cry easily. But this was not choking up. I was weeping, and my mom started to cry too.

Through tears Mom looked at me and said, "Why does it matter so much to you?" In her mind she had done all she could, staying in a less than ideal marriage until the kids were gone. Now she just wanted relief from all the pain.

"I don't know, Mom, it just does," I answered.

I'm not sure if it was my tears that night or for other reasons, but Mom reconsidered her decision. She stayed with my dad, and in the years that followed he started attending Alcoholics Anonymous and quit drinking. His manic-depressive behavior smoothed out. And their marriage improved; it probably became better than it had been since they were newlyweds.

Then a bleeding mole on my dad's back was diagnosed as melanoma, and after just two and a half years, he died. In reflecting later on these events, I was so grateful to God that in his last years Dad not only had an enjoyable relationship with Mom, but he didn't have to suffer and die from cancer living alone. Mom might have been elsewhere, perhaps remarried, wondering if she needed somehow to take care of him. I was so glad they had stuck together to the end.

A few years after losing Dad, my mom moved into a retirement area where a number of single women lived. Mom said to me one day, "I can usually tell without finding out first who the divorced women are. There is a bitterness and hardness in the countenance of their faces."

I thought, *Mom, I am so glad that's not on your face. I am thankful that you took divorce off the table. I am thankful, not only for me, but for my kids. I am thankful you gave us a legacy of faithfulness in marriage.*

WHY GOD WANTS MARRIAGES TO LAST

God takes marriage very seriously, so He desires for all of us to commit ourselves to the kind of legacy my mom and dad left. To accomplish that successfully, we need to understand the passion in God's heart concerning lifelong commitment in marriage.

God is clear in Scripture: He hates divorce. Here are four reasons why I believe God so despises the breaking of a marriage covenant:

God Hates Divorce Because of What It Says About His Character and His Glory

That sounds strange, perhaps, but God loves His own glory. No, He's not an egomaniac; He's just *God*. In fact He put us on earth for the purpose of glorifying Him. The old catechism says, "The chief end of man is to glorify God and to enjoy Him forever." Our purpose for existence is to bring glory to God, and He is supremely satisfied when He is glorified.

The Bible teaches that marriage is a picture of the relationship between Christ and the Church. Has Christ ever abandoned or divorced the Church? Of course not. In fact, God has said, "I will never desert you, nor will I ever forsake you" (Heb. 13:5).

Divorce harms this picture of Christ's relationship with His Church. We do not injure His glory, but to the watching world we mar the picture of His glory. For no other reason than this we should say, "I never want to get a divorce. I don't want to hurt God's reputation." If you love the Lord, if you want to see His name glorified, then divorce must come off the table.

The whole story of the gospel is about a God whose relationship with His bride was broken because of what she did. And God in effect said, "I will do anything; I will move heaven and earth to reconcile that relationship. I will even sacrifice My Son to restore that relationship." That's how God feels about reconciled relationships. In order not to damage and discredit His glory, we must do whatever it takes to heal and preserve our marriage relationship.

God Hates Divorce Because He Loves You

He knows the long-term damage and impact that divorce will have on your life. He knows the pain that will last as long as you live. He knows the bitterness that will well up inside you. He can look ahead to the day when you will go to a high school graduation for one of your children and be seated in one area and your ex-wife or ex-husband will be seated elsewhere. God says, "I love you so much I don't want that for you."

You might be thinking, *Well, if God loves me so much, doesn't He understand the pain I'm going through in my marriage? I think I*

can handle the graduation thing years from now—but I'll never survive this!

God does care deeply about that. Maybe some of the conflict in your relationship now has been engineered by God to force you to deal with issues in your own heart and life that otherwise would go ignored. Pain gets our attention.

You might be thinking, *Surely, I would not have this pain with someone else.* The problem is that if you do not confront the disease in your relationship, guess what? In another marriage the issues will pop right back up. Why do you think the divorce rate is even higher in second marriages than in the first? Because the individuals never dealt with the issues lodged deep in their own hearts. They think, *I just picked the wrong person the first time. If I can find the right one, that will fix everything.*

The other person is probably not the issue. You need to go before the Lord and say, "Search me, try me, examine my heart, Lord. Show me where I need to repent and change."

God Hates Divorce Because He Loves Your Children

A recent article in *Time* magazine was entitled "Should You Stay Together for the Kids?" It told of the studies of divorce effects by Judith Wallerstein, a seventy-eight-year-old researcher at the University of California at Berkeley.

Starting in the 1970s, Wallerstein found young children of divorce and tried to determine what they were going through. She has followed the lives of these children for the last twenty-five years, and in a new book, *The Unexpected Legacy of Divorce*, Wallerstein tells about 131 case studies.

One of the persons studied is named Virginia Gafford, who now is fifty-six years old. Virginia first married when she was nineteen. That marriage lasted three years. Her second marriage produced a child, Denyse, and when Denyse was fourteen, Virginia divorced again. According to Wallerstein, Denyse developed the classic symptoms of children of divorce. Boyfriends jilted her for being too emotionally needy. She longed for the perfect man, but he was nowhere to be found. The *Time* article reports,

> "I had really high expectations," says Denyse. "I wanted Superman, so they wouldn't do what Dad had done." Denyse is in college now and getting fine grades, but her mother still has certain regrets. "If I could go back and find any way to

save that marriage, I'd do it," she says. "And I would tell anyone else to do the same."[1]

Of course our mighty, loving God can heal the wounds in
the hearts of children who grow up in divorced homes. My
wife's parents divorced when she was in high school. God
has done a work in Mary Ann's heart and life to heal many
of those wounds. And if you now are part of a blended family, don't despair! The challenges are often intense, but press
forward to godliness in your life and marriage. God wants to
restore and bless; He will take "the years that the swarming
locust has eaten" (Joel 2:25) and restore them to bring glorious fruit.

But if you are contemplating divorce, is that really what
you want for your children? You might ask, "But won't it be
painful for the kids if we stay together and are not getting
along?"

Yes, it will be—if you don't work on your marriage and do
everything you can to fix the reasons you aren't getting along.
But don't expect divorce to be the magical solution that solves
all of the problems for both the children and adults in your
family.

Researcher Wallerstein says that she used to think that if a
divorcing couple could be civil with one another, if they could
settle the financial issues fairly and both maintain contact with
their children, the kids would be okay and would bounce back.
She has changed her tune, which the *Time* magazine article
made clear:

Besides her conclusions on children's long-term prospects following divorce, Wallerstein makes another major point in her book—one that may result in talk-show fistfights. Here it is: children don't need their parents to like each other. They don't even need them to be especially civil. They need them to stay together, for better or worse. (Paging Dr. Laura!) This imperative comes with asterisks, of course, but fewer than one might think. Physical abuse, substance addiction and other severe pathologies cannot be tolerated in any home. Absent these, however, Wallerstein stands firm: a lousy marriage, at least where the children's welfare is concerned, beats a great divorce.[2]

God hates divorce because He loves your kids and knows the long-term effects it will have on their lives.

God Hates Divorce Because He Loves His Church

As puzzling as it may be, there appears to be more divorce among Christians than in the general population. The Christian pollster George Barna has reported that while 24 percent of people in the culture have experienced a divorce, 27 percent of those who call themselves evangelical Christians have been divorced. The number climbs to 30 percent among those identifying themselves as fundamental Christians.[3] Maybe the trauma of divorce has brought hurting people to church and therefore, statistically, divorce is more represented in the Church than in the general population. But I think experience tells us that when it comes to divorce, there isn't a dramatic difference between what is going on in the Church and what is going on in the culture.

I wonder if one of the reasons for the impotence of the Church today is that we have to use so many resources in caring for so many self-inflicted wounds like divorce. I am not suggesting that we not care for wounded people, but what might we be able to accomplish if those wounds never happened in the first place or were patched up and marriages restored?

God loves His Church and wants it unleashed to be His representative in the culture. He hates divorce for the same reason that you would hate poison in the hand of your children because of what it might do to them. That's why we need to take divorce off the table.

A Marriage That Will Make God Smile

I want to challenge you to make five choices that will not only protect your own marriage but also contribute to the salvation of other marriages to the benefit of the kingdom of God and His glory:

Decide That Divorce Is Not an Option for You

Just take it off the table! Promise to one another not only that you won't get a divorce, but that you won't even threaten it. Don't ever make statements like: "Maybe we would have been better off if we had not gotten married." Words have power, and ones like those can rock the security, the very foundation of your marriage. Repent of them!

Instead of harmful words, speak words of blessing and encouragement and find ways to fix the problems instead of just talking about them.

Change Your Attitude About Divorce in Society

The next time you hear a press report that says two Hollywood stars are getting a divorce but are still "really good friends," see it for what it is—a bunch of public relations baloney. People don't get divorced because they are really good friends and it is just "time for them to move along." Is that what love is all about? A more accurate story probably would be that these

people are fighting all the time and hate each other. But that kind of news does not do much to enhance a film career.

When You See a Friend's Marriage in Danger, Do Something

Treat it like the serious issue that it is. Be willing to confront him or her.

In 1987, I was a groomsman in a wedding. Thirteen years later I got a call from the groom. He told me that his wife was leaving him. I believed I had a responsibility before God as a witness to that wedding, so I called the wife and sent her material. I have spent hours on the phone with the man saying, "Do I need to fly there? I'm involved in marriage ministry. What can I do to help you guys out?"

We have to lay down our lives for people in that situation. The next time you hear about a friend who is thinking of getting a divorce, don't avoid that person! Ask, "What can I do? I will do anything to help you heal your marriage."

Schedule Regular Maintenance for Your Marriage

You would never expect your car to go 200,000 miles without changing the oil, getting tune-ups, and making some repairs from time to time. Is a marriage any different? Invest in regular attention to your most important relationship—date nights, marriage enrichment events like "I Still Do," a FamilyLife Marriage weekend, or a marriage conference at your church. Read books, listen to tapes, or watch videos. Take a weekend away at least once a year and just focus on each other; discuss how the two of you can take your relationship to the next level.

If you discover that something of an overhaul is in order, don't shrink back! Marriage is tough. You may need to spend many hours with a pastor or a counselor to help sort through issues you can't see on your own. But something as valuable as your marriage is well worth the investment.

Help Strengthen and Protect Other Marriages

I'm not talking about marriages in trouble. I'm suggesting you look for ways to do something positive for those marriages that are clipping along smoothly to keep them from hitting a skid. Here's a specific challenge: How about starting a small-group study related to marriage in your neighborhood or with friends at work? It's not that hard; you don't need to be a marriage expert or teacher. All you need is a willingness to get personally involved in helping build covenant marriages in America, and God will do the rest. To help you begin, FamilyLife has an introductory HomeBuilders study that can be downloaded free from the Internet (www.familylife.com), or you can call FamilyLife to receive a printed copy in the mail (1-800-FL-TODAY). The study guide in the Appendix of this book is another possibility for a small-group series.

In particular I want to challenge men to take the lead in starting these groups. Our prayer is that God will use thousands of committed volunteers like you to unleash a nationwide movement so that ten years from now we can look back and say, "See what God has done to turn around the divorce rate!"

If you will make these five choices, you will settle once and for all the foundational issue of commitment and covenant in marriage. But that means taking the option of divorce or abandonment off the table and throwing it in the trash can. You have to decide you are going to do what it takes to stay together from this day forward.

Do what you promised. Keep your vows—no matter what. " 'Til death do us part." For the glory of God!

Bob Lepine is the cohost of the FamilyLife Today *radio program and the author of* The Christian Husband. *He and his wife, Mary Ann, have five children and live in Little Rock, Arkansas.*

12

Build Your Marriage on the Rock

DENNIS RAINEY

The story is told of a wise person who was asked: "Is there any thing more beautiful than a young boy and girl clasping clean hands and pure hearts at the doorway of marriage? Can young love be improved upon?"

The answer is, "Yes!" An even more beautiful spectacle is an old man and woman finishing together on the same path where their journey began. Their hands are gnarled but still clasped. Their faces are seamed but still radiant. Their hearts are worn but still devoted.

Yes, more beautiful than young love is old love.

We all want to arrive at that destination. But what will make the difference in our lives and marriages that will take us the distance "'til death do us part"?

Such a completion may seem impossible to you now. Are you at a crossroads? Are you desperate for help? Are you in relational pain? Has your marriage gone through enormous trial and you wonder about the future? I know where hope is to be found! Psalm 127:1 says, "Unless the LORD builds the house, they labor in vain who build it." Jesus Christ wants to help take your marriage to completion.

But you must first make a foundational choice. Jesus spoke of this decision in a parable in the Sermon on the Mount:

> Therefore everyone who hears these words of Mine, and acts upon them, may be compared to a wise man, who built his house upon the rock. And the rain descended, and the floods came, and the winds blew, and burst against that house; and yet it did not fall, for it had been founded upon the rock. And everyone who hears these words of Mine, and does not act upon them, will be like a foolish man, who built his house upon the sand. And the rain descended, and the floods came, and the winds blew, and burst against that house; and it fell, and great was its fall. (Matt. 7:24–27)

This parable has several notable *couples*: two foundations, sand and rock; two home builders, foolish and wise; two responses, disobedience and obedience; two legacies, devastation and permanence.

The one common ingredient to both of these houses was

trouble—the rain, wind, and flood. There isn't a marriage that won't see storms. Maybe it is the storm of a job loss, an illness, a physical handicap, an emotional problem. Maybe it's a financial disaster or the temptations of too much prosperity. Maybe the foundation of your marriage is being battered by unmet expectations, rebellious children, meddling in-laws. The potential list is long. The question is: What foundation are you building under your house? What will enable you to beat the odds and build a marriage that withstands life's storms?

BUILD AN ENDURING LEGACY

Near the end of a recent meeting at FamilyLife, one of our staff members, Jim, walked up the aisle with a microphone in his hand and began talking. When he reached the second row he dropped down on one knee in front of a young lady and said, "I want to leave a different legacy. Will you be my bride?"

Once we realized what was happening, the entire staff erupted in a standing ovation. We had witnessed a marriage proposal. People were cheering through their tears!

Later I asked Jim, "Why did you say you wanted to leave a different legacy? What was the legacy you were given as a young man?" Instead of an immediate answer, Jim wrote me a three-page explanation. Here's a portion of what he said:

> I have never known the meaning of a real family. My legacy is that of divorce, addictions, and passivity. As I grew up, I

knew that I wanted more out of life than I was getting. I saw other families that were happy and normal. I told myself that that was the kind of father and husband I wanted to be. Every couple of years a new stepmother would come into my life. They all tried to be nice to me but after seeing the first five or six come and go, I knew they wouldn't be around for long. They were nice but I couldn't get close to them because I knew they would be traded in soon for a newer model. The last one was number 15 I think. That marriage lasted six weeks. It was always easier for my father to get a divorce than deal with the issues.[1]

Obviously, that's not how to do marriage! There is no such thing as a good divorce. Divorce begins an emotional earthquake in the lives of two adults and their children that can ripple out to multiple generations. The Bible tells us that the sins of parents who hate God will cause punishment to their descendants for three or four generations (Ex. 20:5). That should sober us about the choices we're making today. It's impossible to predict how many people will be impacted by a single choice like divorce. That is why it is so important to build your house on the rock, by hearing God's instructions and practicing them.

The great *upside* of obedience is that God promises to show love to a thousand generations of those who love Him and keep His commandments (Ex. 20:6). That makes me want to avoid foolishness and stay on the side of pleasing and obeying God's wishes—in marriage and all areas of life.

REPENT OF DIVORCE?

What is your attitude about divorce? Better stated, what is your counsel when a friend or family member lets you know they are thinking of divorce? We live in a culture of divorce. Divorce has become the all too common solution to marital problems, even within the Church. Divorce has become a personal right in the Christian community. It is not only accepted, it is *expected* as an alternative to an unhappy marriage.

I believe it is time that we change our attitude about divorce. I believe the Christian community needs to repent from divorce.

This is a very difficult subject to talk about, and I want to say here that I realize many who read this book have been affected by divorce. Many *are* divorced. We must compassionately speak the truth about divorce. We must love those who are divorced while at the same time holding forth the truth of Scripture. God stated clearly in Malachi 2:16, "For I hate divorce." He didn't say He hated the divorcees, the people of divorce. He hated the *act* of divorce. Why? Because of what it does to adults, children, and a nation.

I believe we must comfort those whose lives have been broken by divorce. We must also unashamedly and unapologetically uphold the standard of Scripture: Divorce is not God's choice for a struggling couple.

I believe that it is time for the Christian community to repent of its lackadaisical, ho-hum attitude about an act that is destroying Christian families. It is time for the Church to repent of its cavalier attitude about divorce. It is time for Christians to rethink their counsel when friends ask for advice.

If God hates divorce, what should we think of it? Many of us are not embracing the act by getting a divorce, but we simply say and do nothing about someone who does. Repentance is a change of mind. It's a 180 degree turn in the opposite direction.

Paul wrote, "For the sorrow that is according to the will of God produces a repentance without regret, leading to salvation; but the sorrow of the world produces death" (2 Cor. 7:10). Repentance can bring life even out of our mistakes, out of our brokenness.

A year or two ago a friend I'll call John told me that after attending an "I Still Do" event, he was on a plane flying home when he began to weep. John had gone through a divorce a number of years before this. He realized after listening to the same series of messages reproduced in this book that he needed to repent from his own divorce and his attitude about divorce and seek healing from the shame he still carried. He said to me, "There are so many of us who need to be released from the mess that divorce creates. My repentance on that plane released me."

John went on to say, "So many of us have never repented over our divorces—the wrong choices, the mistakes, the breaking of our covenant. There are others of us in the Christian community and the Church who need to repent from our attitudes about divorce. It's the grandparents, the parents, the neighbors, and others who all advised their friends and their family members to get a divorce."

His words stunned me. I had never seen so clearly that Christians have become complacent about an act that God was very clear about.

If God hates divorce, what should we *do* about it? I believe we need to begin by repenting (changing our minds) from divorce and then do several things.

First, we need to eliminate the "D word" (divorce) from our vocabulary in our marriages. We need to replace the "D word" with the "C words"—*covenant* and *commitment*. We need to pledge to our spouses, and if need be to our children, that we will never use the "D word" in our marriage. For a Christian, divorce is neither a right nor an option.

Second, we need to change the counsel we give others who want to get a divorce. Instead of telling a family member what may *seem* to be the easiest solution, we need to encourage, implore, and exhort them to find a way to address their problems. My friend Joe will tell you today that he is happily married because he had a brother-in-law who loved him enough to "come after him" and challenge him to keep his commitments. Joe would say that he was on a track to make the worst decision in his life. Tough love, persistent love, didn't let him do it.

Saying nothing. Doing nothing. Those are *not* options for a Christian with a friend who is about to do something he or she will regret later. I wish I could tell you that every couple whom I've *challenged* and *called back* to their covenant is still married. Many went ahead and divorced anyway. And in many cases it resulted in the loss of our friendship. Nonetheless, I urge you to join with many of us in the body of Christ in repenting from the sin of embracing divorce as an acceptable solution. If we are to see the sacred nature of the marriage covenant restored, we must encourage Christians to keep their most holy vow.

GO THE DISTANCE!

Do you want to see your marriage make it to the "old and in love" stage? Here are some ways to help your marriage and the marriages of others go the distance—"'til death do us part."

Pray Together Every Day As a Couple

Twenty-six years ago I was newly married. I knew a man named Carl who was successfully married, so I asked him, "What is the best piece of advice you can give me as a young man who has been married six weeks?"

"Oh, that's easy, Denny," he said. "Pray together every night with your wife."

"Sounds good to me. I'll do it," I said.

I did not realize how powerful that advice was and how it would change the course of my life and my legacy as a man. I started praying regularly with Barbara.

It was easy for a few days until one night I noticed that she was facing one wall and I was facing the opposite wall. Our sleep positions were symbolic of our relationship. We weren't in a praying mood.

There was a tap on the shoulder and it wasn't Barbara. It was the Lord and my conscience: *Rainey, are you going to pray with her tonight?*

In my thoughts I replied, *No, Lord, I don't like her tonight.*

He answered, *I know. That is why you need to pray with her.*

But, Lord, You know that in this situation she is 90 percent wrong.

And it's your 10 percent that caused her to be 90 percent wrong.

Lord, don't bore me with details and facts.

I struggled with God a bit and He said, *But you're the one who tells them at the FamilyLife marriage conferences that you pray with your wife every night.*

That's a cheap shot, Lord.

After more struggling with God, I finally rolled over and

tapped Barbara on the shoulder and said, "Sweetheart, will you forgive me for being 10 percent wrong?"

Just kidding! I didn't say that—or if I did, I only said it once! A one-night spat can last a couple of days if you do that.

No, I rolled over and just as I started to speak, the words stuck in my throat, at that spot they call the Adam's apple. It was so hard to ask her to forgive me when I was feeling self-righteous and so justified in my argument. But I finally got it out: "Sweetheart, will you forgive me?" That was the beginning of working our disagreement through and getting to the point where we could pray together.

I can safely say I don't know if we would still be married if we hadn't had that spiritual discipline of daily prayer together in our marriage.

In addition to tapping into God's wisdom and power through prayer, I believe that the act of prayer involves humility, vulnerability, and surrender, which are hard to do if you are out of fellowship with your prayer partner. Prayer encourages the softening of hard hearts and creates an environment of intimacy and communion.

If you are not praying together daily as a couple, then I urge you to make a commitment to your spouse to begin today.

Solidify Your Vows by Signing a Marriage Covenant

I want to challenge you to sign a covenant and hang it prominently in your home. In the Appendix, we'll show you how.

About two years ago, I was working on an editorial and thinking about what we needed to do to rescue families and stop the moral slide of America. I pushed back from my computer keyboard for a few moments and was praying and pondering when the Lord impressed on me, *Will you stop worrying about the nation and just take care of your own family? Think about it.* All of a sudden it hit me. Our daughter was getting married in about six weeks.

I talked to Barbara about my thoughts, and later we went to Ashley and her fiancé, Michael, and asked them if they would let us take their wedding vows and have a calligrapher write them on parchment. Then during the ceremony, after they had said their vows orally, they would turn to that piece of paper and sign their names in permanent ink. We left room on the document for others to sign as well—witnesses to their covenant of marriage.

They agreed, and that beautiful piece of paper now hangs framed above the fireplace in their home. I am convinced that if their house were on fire, before they even rescued their wedding pictures and other keepsakes, Michael and Ashley would grab that framed covenant. Even in their short marriage, they have already gone back more than once and reread what they promised to each other.

So if you sign and hang your covenant, you will be joining a worldwide movement that I believe is upon God's heart. He wants to redeem marriages—including yours. Marriage is one man and one woman in a covenant relationship with their God for a lifetime. If the details of the covenant are put in writing and displayed for everyone to see, I believe the marriage relationship moves to a higher level of accountability—as we saw in the touching story I shared in Chapter 1.

If you are a pastor or layperson active in leadership of a local church, why not consider having an annual covenant-signing ceremony as part of a marriage/family emphasis in your church? A number of churches across America are doing this and receiving an enthusiastic response. This is a great way to encourage couples on a yearly basis to renew their vows and say, "We still do." My colleague and friend Bob Lepine has said on our radio broadcast, "We pledge allegiance to the flag hundreds of times in our lifetime and think nothing of it. Restating our vows is a way we can *re-pledge* our allegiance to marriage on an annual basis."

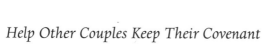

Help Other Couples Keep Their Covenant

Every couple needs a mission. You can take the bread of hope for the family to others. I enthusiastically endorse what Bob Lepine said in the previous chapter—I challenge you to consider leading a home study related to marriage and family topics. You can make a difference in saving marriages and families in America by working for the number one "home builder" in the world—God!

Do What You Promised

In a word, be faithful and persevere. I love what C. H. Spurgeon, the great English preacher, once said: "It was by perseverance that the snail reached the ark." I have always taken great hope from that because I was never the fastest man on the track. I am still not the fastest in many things I do today in life. But God gave me a heart to never quit. And when it comes to your marriage I believe He has given you the same attitude. You don't have to be perfect. You just need to persevere and not give up.

You may have heard of Robertson and Muriel McQuilken, who live in Columbia, South Carolina. For twenty-two years, Robertson served as the president of Columbia Bible College and Seminary. Muriel was always his biggest fan and supporter, but in 1984, her health began to deteriorate because of Alzheimer's disease. Muriel lost some of her speech skills. Her reasoning failed, and she couldn't feed or dress herself. She sometimes wandered away from home and got lost in their neighborhood.

In 1990, Robertson assembled the college's student body and announced his resignation as president so that he could stay at home and care for Muriel, his wife of more than forty years. Here are some of the words Robertson spoke that day. I think you will agree that they are powerful in expressing the true meaning of a lasting marriage covenant.

I have in my life experienced easy decision-making on major decisions, but one of the simplest I have had to make is this one because circumstances dictated it. Muriel, in the last couple of months, seems to be *almost* happy when with me, and *almost never* happy when not with me. In fact, she seems to feel trapped, becomes very fearful, sometimes almost terrified, and when she can't get to me, there can be anger and distress. But when I am with her, she is happy and contented.

And so I must be with her at all times, and you see it is not only because I promised in sickness and in health 'til death do us part—and I am a man of my word. But I have said publicly, [staying with her is] the only fair thing because she has sacrificed for me for forty years to make my life possible. So if I cared for her for forty years, I would still be indebted.

However, it is not that I have to, but I get to. I love her very dearly . . . She is a delight.[2]

Barbara was standing in the laundry room of our home ironing when I called from the office and read her the story of Robertson and Muriel McQuilken. She ended up watering the clothes with her tears.

I asked her, "Should I tell that story in my talks?"

Quietly, she choked back an answer and a question, "Yes, but I do have one question. I need to know if you love me like that?"

"Yes," I said.

There's not a woman who doesn't want to know the answer to that question from her husband. And there's not a man who would not want to hear the same thing from his wife—"Yes, I will love you like that." It is what we long for. It is a demonstration of commitment and covenant. It is what we all deeply want and need because God built it in us.

Will you join Barbara and me on the journey to completing a covenant marriage?

Dennis Rainey is executive director of FamilyLife and a sought-after speaker who has spoken at PromiseKeepers, the annual assembly of the Southern Baptist Convention, and Amsterdam 2000. He is the author or coauthor of a number of books including One Home at a Time, The Tribute and the Promise, *and* Building Your Mate's Self-Esteem. *With Barbara he has coauthored* Starting Your Marriage Right, Parenting Today's Adolescent, *and* Moments Together for Couples. *The Raineys are parents of six children and live near Little Rock, Arkansas.*

13

Marriage Covenant Memories and Ceremonies

DENNIS AND BARBARA RAINEY

The "I Still Do" arena events have brought many exciting and rewarding outcomes; thousands of marriages have been saved, improved, and encouraged. Every couple has a story to tell, and in this chapter we will share some of those we have received at FamilyLife.

We will also list some of the creative ways husbands and wives have chosen to renew their vows through a marriage covenant-signing ceremony.

Finally, we will give several reports from churches across America where the corporate church body has gathered to celebrate marriage through vow renewal and covenant-signing events. Truly, a movement is under way in our land to take back ground that has been lost! The high and holy covenant of marriage is once again receiving the honor it is due in the Church. Praise be to God!

If you have a story of your own you would like to share, or if you are a pastor who has led a covenant renewal ceremony in your church—or would like to, please send us an E-mail through our Web site at www.familylife.com.

"I Still Do" Memories

Here in their own words, with editing for length and style, are some reports from couples who attended "I Still Do." We thank each one for taking the time to share their story.

S

We recently attended the "I Still Do" conference in D.C. What a powerful day that was!

That day a wish I've had for a few years came true. A few years back, I told my husband that for our tenth anniversary I would like to renew our vows, which were originally taken on May 6, 1989.

He, being him, said that once was sufficient and he meant them then and now and there was no need to go through the hoopla again. To which I replied, "But it would mean even more now—we've grown a lot since then!" Little did I know what the Lord had planned for us both.

As we stood there at the end of the seminar on Saturday and said our vows again, my heart almost burst with the understanding that the Lord knows and loves us and desires so much of the best things for His children. And as I stood there and watched (and wept . . . a lot of weeping) while my dearly beloved said his vows to me (with tears in his eyes), I realized how much he and I *still do.*

—E-mail from Washington, D.C.

My husband was in the throes of a new medical career and I was an RN with an erratic professional schedule. We allowed "life" to get in the way of the spiritual commitment we had made to God for our marriage.

Our marriage did not suffer infidelity, addiction, or threats of divorce. But I think we both felt very sad that it was so empty. We had a difficult time relating to each other. This gnawed on us for years, despite the blessings of financial success and two beautiful and healthy children.

Jeff was trying to help make our marriage and family work better. In July of 1994, he gave up a very successful (and lucrative) solo Ob/Gyn [obstetrics/gynecology] practice that he had built. He is now home most nights with the kids and we are active members of our church and Sunday school—together!

God has used this past year to turn our marriage back toward Him. On Valentine's Day my husband gave me a letter reclaiming the spiritual leadership of our home. And on July 15, we attended the "I Still Do" conference in Baltimore. With our hearts rekindled and in harmony with God, we renewed our vows.

I now know that perfection is not the goal for our marriage, nor is it even possible. Rather, marriage is a process and one that must include Christ so that we can follow His ultimate journey for us as a couple and family. The "I Still Do" conference was able to take our marriage to an additional level in this process of reclaiming a union that is pleasing to God . . . and for this, we are forever grateful!

—C. W.

[This next letter is from a woman who attended "I Still Do" for educational purposes and placed this message on the familylife.com Web site.]

I was not a Christian during my marriage, so all this comes after a divorce.

Since I am now single, it was very difficult for me to turn and face my partner [at "I Still Do"]. I don't have one. The only person I had there to make those commitments/vows to was Jesus Christ Himself. I wrote a little note to myself in my notepad that I will have placed on a gold plaque and attached to the covenant; it goes something like this: "Until the day comes that God provides me that perfect gift called a husband, I make these vows to Jesus Christ Himself. If that day never comes, then I will have had the most perfect Husband that could have ever been given."

§⤳

I attended "I Still Do" with my wife in Washington, D.C., in July 1999. I went there for my wife. However, I saw husbands and wives holding hands and showing their love and appreciation for each other. I had not ever really been exposed to that other than dating. So I felt out of place at first. Then as time went on I realized that my wife was a gift from God and that it was okay to hold hands and tell her that I love her—it really feels good!

I couldn't wait to share this with my stepson and tell him that I will never leave his mother. In fact, I told him that I want to share with him how much this marriage covenant means.

We have been walking/sometimes stumbling with the Lord for almost ten years. I have always loved my wife—I just didn't tell her or show her enough. So I thank you very much. In fact, I thank you so much that we are going to share this with other couples and let them know that we say *no* to divorce.

I want to leave a true, lasting legacy in our home and pray that others will too.

—Letter from Washington, D.C.

Marriage Covenant Ceremony
Ideas and Memories

At "I Still Do" we give each couple in attendance an attractive, oversize, framable marriage covenant. We encourage all couples to go home and find some creative way to observe and celebrate the actual signing and witnessing of the covenant. Here are some stories of what couples have done.

The date of the "I Still Do" conference was in October, and our anniversary is in November. Right after the conference—before going home—we went together and bought a frame.

Later, we had our preacher (who is my husband's prayer partner/ friend) and his wife over to the house and we, along with our children (from a previous marriage), renewed our vows.

We wanted the kids there because when my husband married me, he knew it was a *package deal*. (He asked them for permission to marry me!) We signed the covenant and had our friends (preacher and wife) sign it. It now hangs in our living room. We plan on redoing our vows every five years, and taking down the covenant and signing and dating it each time.

We are extremely blessed in our marriage and all the credit for that goes to God! What a praise! There are three *threads/ strands* in our marriage—my husband, God, and me!

—B. K.

Since both of our college-age children are out of the area for the summer months, we want to wait until a weekend when they are both home to have them as our witnesses. My husband plans on having the frame ready and the place prepared so we can hang it right after the signatures are completed. We want a candlelight dinner and a small wedding cake to celebrate too.

—FamilyLife.com posting, July 1999

[A young man posted this reply:]

I just want to affirm what an impact the signing will be for your college-age children. I myself am twenty-one and know the importance of knowing the marriage *works*. My generation is scarred by divorce. Knowing that our parents love each other with a God-embraced commitment is an incredible witness to us. What a legacy you are leaving!

We took our marriage covenant to Nevada where we visited friends. The husband of this couple was one of our groomsmen in our wedding. He and his wife each took turns reading the covenant aloud while my husband and I faced each other and repeated what was said. It was so special; many tears were shed. We had them sign and date the covenant as witnesses. We're getting it framed to hang on our wall so we can see it every day.

—FamilyLife.com posting, July 1999

𝒮𝒶

[The marriage covenant ceremony] wasn't original to us, but we decided to have a dinner party with our closest friends and sign it in their presence. We sent out formal invitations and nine of the ten people invited were able to attend. We were excited, and the guests were somewhat intrigued about the idea.

We had a lovely evening. We had appetizers, then a formal dinner. After that we stayed at the table and we asked how the couples had been brought together—and what had sealed their decision to marry. It was interesting that though we had known them all for several years, we heard many new things that night. Lots of laughter and a few tears followed. It was very moving for us.

Carl and I were the last couple to give our testimony. Then we read the vows, signed the document, and had our guests sign it also as our witnesses to hold us accountable.

We also noted that no one from our marriage nineteen years prior had been invited, and that these guests that night would be the ones we would invite now. I think it was a powerful night for us all, and we got that feedback as well.

Our beautifully matted and framed covenant hangs over

our bed. At first we thought it would be in a more public place, but then decided to put it in our room, for it is precious to us.

One footnote: Though we have three children, at that time ranging in age from six to fourteen, we decided to have this as an adult evening. I think the children might have felt awkward with some of the emotions. As they get older I'm sure we'll have opportunities to discuss this with them.

—K. M.

We have been married for thirteen years and have become best friends in spite of hard times. We have family scattered across the United States and were trying to find a way to have each family member witness the renewal of our marriage covenant and sign the covenant certificate given at the conference. Our hearts were tremendously burdened for a brother and sister-in-law who had filed for divorce after approximately eighteen years of marriage with two teenagers at home.

Well, God does work in mysterious ways. On October 30,

1999, our seventeen-year-old daughter was killed in a single-car accident. This brought many of our family and friends to the funeral, including our brother and sister-in-law. Our church prepared a luncheon for everyone after the funeral service, and we used this opportunity to renew our covenant and have each person there sign the covenant certificate. We know that God worked on the hearts of our brother and sister-in-law, and they have now decided to drop the divorce proceeding and continue with counseling.

Praise God! I hope that someone will be encouraged by this story and know that even in times of grief, the Lord is able to use the witness of His people for good.

—T. W.

We planned, with our friends, to renew our marriage covenant at the Annual All-Church Retreat just two weeks [after the "I Still Do" conference]. I say "renew" our marriage covenant, but when we were married the ceremony was performed by a nondenominational minister whom we did not know well and the vows were very modern—no mention of submission and a promise to be partners to each other. (Sounds kind of like a business contract, doesn't it?) So for us, the marriage covenant really was a commitment of our marriage to the authority of God and to each other—even to the full meaning of *submission*—without hesitation.

On Saturday, November 7, 1999, we had a marriage

covenant ceremony at Camp Allen, a property of the Episcopal Diocese of Texas located in the East Texas Piney Woods.

God was surely smiling on all of us! Six other couples at the retreat decided to join us in renewing their vows. Some of them we had just met and some were old and dear friends—all are even more special to us now. The ceremony was presided over by our deacon, Thomas H. Murray III, and George S. Thompson of Christian Counselors of Houston.

The ceremony was performed in the late afternoon at the altar by the lake—we call it "Cathedral in the Pines." Afterward, we signed the marriage covenant certificate and had an extra piece of paper for everyone else to witness it for us.

I have started working in stained glass and am planning to create a frame for the certificate with the witness signatures on the back. We are going to hang it in our front hall or maybe even on the front porch for all to see as they approach our door. I have the verse "As for me and my house, we will serve the LORD" (Joshua 24:15) stenciled on our living room wall. Perhaps we will hang it near there. Anyway, it will be prominently displayed in our home and will surely be an heirloom for our children.

—A. S.

After the "I Still Do" conference in San Jose, California, this past summer, two couples from Vacaville, California, formed two separate HomeBuilders groups using the study "Keeping

Your Covenant." The two groups were split into the Young Marrieds (those married five years or less) and those that have a few more years behind them. The studies were exciting and sometimes intense as couples opened up with each other, in many cases for the first time in years. Each couple developed a closer relationship with their spouse along with new and lasting friendships with the other couples.

We culminated the classes by bringing the couples together for a recommitment ceremony at our local church, complete with the marriage covenant certificates.

What made this group somewhat unique was one couple who were separated from each other because of family illness. The wife, who is handicapped and bound to a wheelchair, went back to Michigan to tend to her ailing mother. Her husband called her each week during the class and they went through the studies over the telephone. She said it was her bright spot each week. This couple, during the recommitment ceremony, recited their vows to each other while three thousand miles apart.

We were excited to be a small part in working with these couples and helping them open up to the Lord and each other in ways that they hadn't done before.

—R. & S. K.

Dale and I renewed our vows in celebration of our tenth wedding anniversary on a balmy, unseasonably warm

Saturday afternoon, December 4, 1999. Now, one might say, "It's only been ten years!" But for this second-marriage-for-both blended family, ten years is like twenty-five to any other marriage. We beat all the odds, all the statistics that predicted we wouldn't make it.

We learned that the success of our marriage impacts so many others than merely we two. Of course it impacts our children (who have both already witnessed the fallout of their original family and don't need to see that again), but it also makes an impression on the neighbor down the street, the coworker, the hurting family in the church, the children's friends' parents . . . This marriage-against-the-odds succeeding for eleven years tells the world, "You can make it with God at the wheel. God's got a plan for marriages. And when marriages fail, families fail. When families fail, society fails." No one had ever told us how we are living a legacy—right now, today. That our marriage will make an impact on our grandchildren one day. That was a truly mind-boggling concept to discover.

We renewed our vows in a turn-of-the-century Victorian home.

Dale wore a tuxedo and I wore a floor-length simple ivory gown. We had a small group of our close friends and family, and our pastor, Mark Evans, whom we'd asked one year in advance, led us through our self-written words. The day of our ceremony was the eleventh anniversary of the day that we fell in love on a long walk on a fall Sunday afternoon in Maumelle Park. We spent the rest of the weekend at our original honeymoon location, the same place where he proposed to me at sunset on the cliff.

Our vow-renewal service was highlighted by an exchange of dried olive branches (small, leafy twigs) that signified our choice to forgive, receive forgiveness, and start fresh. We exchanged our original wedding rings all over again. We played Ralph Vaughan Williams's stunningly beautiful piece "The Lark Ascending" as background music. We signed, with our pastor, the FamilyLife marriage covenant.

We can truly say that our vow renewal held deeper meaning to both of us than our wedding day did. We love each other more today than we did when we married. It is less of a physical, emotional love and more of a commitment and respect now.

—M. A. G.

Marriage Covenant and Vow Renewal Services in Churches

We know that only a small number of couples will ever make it to an "I Still Do" event. But most Christian couples attend a local church. One of our dreams is that thousands of churches in America and throughout the world will hold a marriage vow or covenant renewal ceremony every year. In addition to a very positive impact on individual marriages, such an annual event will bring needed honor to the institution of marriage. This could become a major weapon in turning the tide in our time against divorce and the deterioration of the family.

Although "I Still Do" is now "officially" an event sponsored by FamilyLife, the first "I Still Do" event I am aware of actually took place at a local church. We begin with this story and then conclude with other reports of similar ceremonies.

A full two years before an "I Still Do" arena event, Steve Campbell, the leader of a young couples' Sunday school class at Markham Street Baptist Church in Little Rock, Arkansas, decided to hold a marriage vow renewal ceremony for his class. He called the event "I Still Do"—the same title as a contemporary romantic song.

The entire wedding experience was re-created for about thirty couples. The evening began with a catered meal—the *rehearsal dinner*—at a site away from the church. The men wore coats and ties and the women fancy dresses.

After the dinner the group returned to the church, which had been decorated as for a wedding with flowers and candelabras. The music played as each couple came down the aisle.

A pastor then led everyone through a vow renewal ceremony.

At a point in the service each couple signed a personal covenant as well as a covenant document designed for the entire group. The collective covenant later was framed and hung permanently in the room where the Sunday school class meets.

A reception followed the ceremony, complete with wedding cake and a fountain of punch. A photographer took pictures of each couple.

Steve reports that the event was very successful and has had a lasting impact. One "bride" wrote later that although she had not really understood or meant her vows at her wedding, at the renewal ceremony she "really meant them." She noted that from this point on she and her husband planned to observe their wedding anniversary on the date of the renewal ceremony—not their wedding date.

Another woman wrote Steve saying that since her first wedding was done with little ceremony by a justice of the peace, she now viewed the church's vow renewal event as her *real* wedding.

Steve says that the only thing he would change to make the event even better would be to do some formal teaching on the meaning of the marriage covenant beforehand.

Here are some letters with other examples of church covenant renewal services:

We had a Covenant Marriage Sunday, which was the last installment for a monthlong emphasis. I taught several lessons: "You May Not Like This Lesson If You're a Husband,"

"You May Not Like This Lesson If You're a Wife," and "How to Have a Miracle Marriage."

The Covenant Marriage Sunday did not have a lesson but featured a ceremony for the couples. It became very crowded around the platform—an awesome sight! At two worship services, a total of about 725 renewed their vows. Some invited their friends and relatives.

The church provided a certificate to every couple that signed. A professional photographer took a portrait of every couple participating, which was given to each couple as a gift from their church.

The pastor and his wife's own portrait and certificate were displayed in the lobby for four weeks prior to the Covenant Marriage Ceremony.

—Senior Pastor Dale Wicker and Pastor Johnny Lewis
First Baptist Church, Conway, Arkansas

Our church had a vow-renewal service in February 2000. The church offered the ceremony off-campus, and it was a beautifully decorated, emotional event. The majority of married couples in the church participated. Advance promotion definitely contributed to the event's success. Children of the couples were included and encouraged to sign the covenants with their parents.

—Senior Pastor Ron Pledger
First Baptist Church, Gainesville, Virginia

The marriage covenant was featured as a two-part seminar and vow renewal service. The pastor and his wife led a marriage seminar on a Saturday, then the couples participated in a vow renewal service on Sunday. Any married couple was invited to participate on Sunday, even if they had not attended the Saturday seminar. About twenty-five couples renewed their vows, and the entire church was positive about the event.

—Pastor Richard Croxton
Braddock Baptist Church, Alexandria, Virginia

In September of 2000, we had eighteen couples renew their vows. The format was just like a large wedding, followed by a grand reception. It was the most wonderful and beautiful occasion. The wives were stunning, as some wore wedding gowns while others wore less formal outfits. All of the men wore black tuxedos. Each couple was allowed ten guests (for the reception) and had sent out formal invitations. At least three hundred were in attendance at the ceremony. The ceremony was outstanding as the ministers offered expressions for the renewal of vows and the blessing of the rings. At the reception, each couple was presented to the audience. Then they signed their covenant, which was placed in a beautiful frame before the end of the reception. Couples who participated had been married from ten to forty-eight years. (The couples had to have been married at least ten years to participate.) It was truly a memorable occasion.

—Pastor Wayne Robinson
Mount Hope Baptist Church, Fredericksburg, Virginia

§➤

Although our church (Fellowship Bible Church, Northwest Arkansas) is very marriage and family oriented, we had not had any service to encourage couples to renew their vows or sign a wedding covenant. We brought this idea to the elders and pastoral staff and they were most supportive.

On a Sunday in October, the two of us shared a message in the morning worship services on the topic of covenant. As a conclusion, one of our teaching pastors, Robert Cupp, led us in a renewal of our vows. Then all couples that wanted to do the same thing were invited to come back that night for a special vow renewal and covenant signing service. We encouraged them to bring their children and anyone else who would appreciate and support such a ceremony.

That night about 225 couples came to renew their vows. Pastor Cupp gave a brief message and once again we shared what the marriage covenant meant to us. Then Pastor Cupp and his wife recited their vows. Next, he asked all couples to stand and he led the entire group in a public recitation of vows.

Ahead of time we had ordered a large quantity of the same covenants used at "I Still Do" events. After the ceremony the couples were invited to meet in the foyer with individual pastors and elders to have their covenants signed and witnessed.

One other idea was very meaningful. A door was erected in a special freestanding frame in the foyer. Every couple that participated was given a covenant card for signing that read "until death do us part." They then hammered the card with a nail onto the door. This was intended to resemble what Martin Luther did when he hammered his theses on the church door at Wittenberg. The door was soon covered with cards, and it will remain on display in the church foyer as a monument reminding us of "Marriage Covenant Sunday." We are hoping there will be such a Sunday every year from now on.

—Jim and Anne Arkins

A Word in Closing

The marriage covenant ceremony can take on many different forms depending on the people involved, the needs of the church and the community, and the context of the ministry. But one thing remains consistent in every ceremony: Lives are changed. Marriages are renewed and reinforced. Couples are reminded that the vows they took on that wedding day years ago mean even more today. And they are able to look at each other with love in their hearts and a steadfast commitment in their souls as they prove the words, "We still do."

Organizing a "We Still Do" Study Group

As with the marriage covenant ceremony, a study series can take on a number of forms depending on the needs of the group. The organization of this book lends itself easily to six class sessions, which could be conducted with an existing Sunday school class or offered as a small-group study option. These six sessions could also be incorporated into a retreat for couples—to get away for a marriage enrichment weekend. Feel free to adapt these six lessons into whatever format will minister best to your group.

Participants should keep a journal in which to write their

responses to questions. They must also commit from the first meeting that they will read the chapters and *Scripture References*, attend the sessions, participate in *Group Discussions*, and complete the *Special Assignments* between meetings. It is recommended that each session conclude with a time of prayer and sharing together as time permits.

We Still Do

CONTENT FOCUS: Chapter 1
Scripture References:
Jeremiah 29:11–14; Matthew 19:4–6

Group Discussion:

1. This is your first session as a group, so begin by introducing yourselves and sharing a brief history of your marriage (how many years married, number and ages of children, other significant facts about your life together). If time permits, share a brief description of the way your lives came together as a couple and what your wedding day was like.

2. Share with each other your expectations for this group study. Why are you participating in this study? What would you like to gain from a series of lessons on the covenant of marriage?

3. Read aloud Jeremiah 29:11–14, then review the story of Melanie and Larry in Chapter 1. What did this verse of Scripture say to Melanie in her time of need? What does it say to us?

4. Read aloud Matthew 19:4–6. What is the "cause" referred to in verse 5? Take a few minutes and discuss your thoughts about why God chose to institute marriage for men and women. Why create the marriage covenant?

What does marriage teach us about our relationship with God?

Special Assignments:

1. Read Chapters 2 and 3 and the Scripture references listed for Session Two.

2. Make a list of what you would consider the "dos and don'ts" of marriage as intended by God. List those things that you know make a marriage work and those things that can destroy it.

3. Look up the word *covenant* in a dictionary and write down the definition given.

"I TAKE YOU . . .

CONTENT FOCUS: Chapters 2–3
Scripture References:
Genesis 2:18–23; 15:1–11, 17–18;
Malachi 2:5–7, 9, 14–17; Hebrews 11:8–10

Group Discussion:

1. Compile a group list of the marriage "dos and don'ts" to prepare the way for upcoming sessions. Keep this list posted as you work through the upcoming sessions and continue to add or delete from the list as you meet and learn.

2. Share your definitions of *covenant*, then read aloud Genesis 15:1–11 and 17–18. According to Hebrew custom, the tradition of dividing animal carcasses and then passing between them was to say, in effect, "If I break this covenant which I have made with you, may the same thing happen to me that has happened to these creatures." In this story, who actually passes between the carcasses in the making of this covenant? What is the significance of this fact? What does this say about God's view of covenant?

3. According to Rod Cooper, what are the four principles that will help us to "embrace, enjoy, and preserve" our marriage covenant? Why does understanding these principles make

such a difference in the day-to-day living out of the marriage covenant?

4. As Joseph Stowell wrote, every husband and wife needs to get in the "covenant mode" by willingly and purposefully meeting the needs of their spouse. Take turns sharing examples of how your partner has demonstrated "covenant mode" actions. As a group list ways everyone—with Christ's help—can increasingly stay in the "covenant mode."

Special Assignments:

1. Read Chapters 4 and 5 and the Scripture references listed for Session Three.

2. Take a moment to write down your thoughts about the roles of husbands and wives. How are they different? How are they the same?

3. Look up the word *submission* in the dictionary and write down the definition.

SESSION THREE:
"To Be My Husband or Wife . . .

CONTENT FOCUS: *Chapters 4–5*
Scripture References:
Genesis 2:24–25; Proverbs 3:5–6; 18:22;
Matthew 28:18; Ephesians 5:22–25; James 4:7–8

Group Discussion:

1. The concept of *submission* is one of the most sensitive topics to address in any discussion about marriage. Take a couple of minutes to share your dictionary definitions of the word. Then discuss why this term is so often perceived negatively when it is applied to the wife's role in marriage.

2. Read aloud Ephesians 5:22–25. What is the love of a husband for his wife compared to? How did Christ show His love for His bride, the Church? How does the Church demonstrate its submission to Christ?

3. What are the two ways that Crawford Loritts says husbands are to love their wives? Karen Loritts writes candidly about her personal struggle in understanding submission in her role as a wife. What did she learn?

4. What challenge does Steve Farrar issue for husbands? How would you expand upon this? What challenge does he likewise issue for wives, and what might you add?

Special Assignments:

1. Read Chapters 6 through 8 and the Scripture references listed for Session Four.

2. List the five *languages of love* as defined by Gary Chapman. Rank these languages using the numbers *1–5*, with *1* representing what *you* feel is the most meaningful language for you, *2* representing the second most meaningful, and so on. Then use the same ranking system to indicate which language is the most meaningful to your *spouse*, second most meaningful, and so on. Take a few moments during the week to compare your lists with your spouse's lists and see how close you both were to each other's responses. What have you learned about each other? How will this affect your relationship?

"TO LOVE, HONOR, AND CHERISH . . .

CONTENT FOCUS: *Chapters 6–8*
Scripture References:
1 Corinthians 13; Ephesians 4:26;
Philippians 2:3; 4:8; Colossians 3:12–14

Group Discussion:

1. What are the steps that Gary Chapman lists for dealing with conflict? Read aloud 1 Corinthians 13. How should this chapter, often called "the love chapter," address the issue of conflict in our relationships?

2. Create a two-column chart and, using the conversation between Gary and Barbara Rosberg, list the comparisons and contrasts they give between men and women. Take a moment to add a few more of your own. How do these differences inevitably lead to occasional conflicts?

3. When a marriage has undergone the stress of conflict, what are the three recommendations the Rosbergs give for rebuilding lost trust?

4. List the four *germs* and the three *antidotes* described by Gary Smalley. Discuss why the given antidotes are so effective in knocking out the germs that can infect a marriage.

Special Assignments:

1. Read Chapters 9 and 10 and the Scripture references listed for Session Five.

2. Think about the two or three most sexually satisfying encounters you and your spouse have enjoyed since your wedding day. What made these interludes so special?

3. If you could change or improve anything about your sexual relationship with your spouse, what would it be? Have you spoken about this with your spouse? If not, why not? If so, how was it received?

"TO HAVE AND TO HOLD . . .

CONTENT FOCUS: Chapters 9–10
Scripture References:
Genesis 1:27–28; Proverbs 5:15–21;
Song of Solomon; Ephesians 5:28–29

Group Discussion:

1. What does Dan Allender list as the three enemies to sexual intimacy? How can we counteract these enemies in our marriages?

2. The Song of Solomon is certainly a departure from what we might consider traditional Scripture. Why do you suppose this love poetry has been included in the Old Testament alongside the historical records and the words of the prophets?

3. According to Tim and Darcy, what are the four purposes of sex within marriage? According to Proverbs 5:15–21 and Ephesians 5:28–29, why is it so important that we work toward building a pleasurable sexual relationship with our mate?

4. What are the three dimensions to sexual intimacy? Take a few minutes to discuss ways that husbands and wives can enhance these various dimensions in their relationship.

   Note: This is the next to the last session, so you may want to spend some time finalizing plans for a Marriage

Covenant Ceremony, which is recommended as a conclusion to this course of study. Specifically, your group will need to decide where and when the ceremony will be held, how the covenants will be prepared for signatures, what frames will be provided, and other details for this special event. Remember that this ceremony should reflect the character and needs of your group. You may want to go ahead and refer to Chapter 13 for ideas so that you too can be creative in planning this special event.

Special Assignments:

1. Read Chapters 11 through 13 and the Scripture references listed for Session Six.

2. Make a list of all of your family members and close friends who have been through a divorce or married someone who had previously been divorced. Next, write down the names of anyone you know who is in the process of going through a divorce or for whom you suspect divorce is an impending possibility. What conclusions do you draw as you look at this list?

3. Now make a totally different list. Write down the names of any couples you know who have had the long-lasting kind of marriage. List those for whom the phrase "I do" has obviously meant, "'til death do us part." What do you think has been the "secret" to these successful marriages?

"'Til Death Do Us Part"

CONTENT FOCUS: *Chapters 11–13*
Scripture References:
Psalm 127:1; Matthew 7:24–27;
2 Corinthians 7:9–10; Hebrews 13:5

Group Discussion:

1. What reasons does Bob Lepine give for God's hating divorce? What are some of the negative effects you have seen from divorce? Can God redeem a life broken by the pain of divorce?

2. What are the five choices Lepine suggests will help save marriages to the benefit of God's kingdom? Will you respond differently now when you hear about a friend considering divorce?

3. Review Matthew 7:24–27. What are the *floods* and *winds* that often blow against our marriages? What are the four steps that Dennis Rainey suggests will help us build our marriages "on the rock"?

4. According to Psalm 127:1, who must ultimately build "the house"? Who must ultimately guard "the city"? So who must ultimately build and guard our marriages?

Special Assignments:

1. How many years have you and your spouse been married? And now the important question: How many *more* years do you intend to remain husband and wife? In light of what you have learned in the past six sessions, what will you need to do to make your marriage successful all those years together?

2. Sit down with your spouse, take a few moments to pray together, and then discuss your answers to these questions. The *great news* is that with God's strength and guidance, you too can have a fulfilling, glorious marriage "as long as you both shall live." God brought you together, He joined you together, and "what therefore God has joined together let no man separate" (Matt. 19:6).

Appendix:

Your Covenant-Signing Ceremony

We think every couple should experience the joy and unforgettable memories of a covenant-signing ceremony. How you choose to do this can be as creative and unique as your original marriage ceremony. Many choose a special moment in their history as a couple—the wedding anniversary, the day of their first date, Valentine's Day. Or it may be done best at a time when the extended family or friends are gathered for a holiday or birthday celebration. Some couples will want to participate as part of a larger covenant-signing ceremony at church or in their small-group Bible study. The options are limitless.

It is important, though, to have the covenant reproduced on paper. You may copy and enlarge the covenant shown on pages 206–8 of this book, order a covenant from the FamilyLife resource center (1-800-FL-TODAY), hire a calligrapher, or have the text typeset at a local print shop. Be sure to use a good quality paper that will last.

After the signing ceremony, put the covenant in a frame and hang it prominently in your home as a daily reminder of your commitment to a marriage that will last a lifetime.

Here is a simple ceremony for the formal signing of your marriage covenant:

THE CEREMONY

Prologue (to be read by husband or wife or both):
Believing that God, in His wisdom and providence, has established marriage as a covenant relationship, a sacred and lifelong promise, reflecting our unconditional love for one another and believing that God intends for the marriage covenant to reflect His promise to never leave us nor forsake us, we, the undersigned, do hereby reaffirm our solemn pledge to fulfill our marriage vows. Furthermore, we pledge to exalt the sacred nature and permanence of the marriage covenant by calling others to honor and fulfill their marriage vows.

Husband's Covenant Vow (to be read by the husband):
In the presence of God and these witnesses, and by a holy covenant, I, _____, (husband's name) joyfully receive you as God's perfect gift for me, to have and to hold from this day forward, for better, for worse, for richer, for poorer, in sickness and in health, to love you, to honor you, to cherish you and to protect you, forsaking all others as long as we both shall live.

Wife's Covenant Vow (to be read by the wife):
In the presence of God and these witnesses, and by a holy covenant, I, _____, (wife's name) joyfully receive you as God's perfect gift for me, to have and to hold from this day forward, for better, for worse, for richer, for poorer, in sickness and in health, to love you, to honor you, to respect and submit to you, forsaking all others as long as we both shall live.

Signing (both husband and wife sign a printed version of the covenant, followed by the signing of the covenant by the witnesses present)

Our Marriage Covenant:
Believing that God, in His wisdom and providence, has established marriage as a covenant relationship, a sacred and lifelong promise, reflecting our unconditional love for one another and believing that God intends for the marriage covenant to reflect His promise to never leave us nor forsake us, we, the undersigned, do hereby reaffirm our solemn pledge to fulfill our marriage vows. Furthermore, we pledge to exalt the sacred nature and permanence of the marriage covenant by calling others to honor and fulfill their marriage vows.

§➤

In the presence of God and these witnesses, and by a holy covenant, I, _____, (husband's name) joyfully receive you as God's perfect gift for me, to have and to hold from this day forward, for better, for worse, for richer, for poorer, in sickness and in health, to love you, to honor you, to cherish you and protect you, forsaking all others as long as we both shall live.

_____ *Husband's Signature*

§➤

In the presence of God and these witnesses, and by a holy covenant, I, _____, (wife's name) joyfully receive you as God's perfect gift for me, to have and to hold from this day forward, for better, for worse, for richer, for poorer, in sickness and in health, to love you, to honor you, to respect and submit to you, forsaking all others as long as we both shall live.

_____ *Wife's Signature*

§➤

Witnessed this day, _____, 20____

_____ *Witness*
_____ *Witness*

§➤

Unless the LORD *builds the house,*
They labor in vain who build it.
(Psalm 127:1)

Notes

CHAPTER 6: SPEAKING LOVE'S LANGUAGES

1. Dorthy Tennov, *Love and Limerence: The Experience of Being in Love* (Chelsea, MI: Scarborough House, 1989).

CHAPTER 8: KILL THOSE RELATIONSHIP GERMS

1. John M. Gottman and Nan Silver, *The Seven Principles for Making Marriage Work* (New York: Crown Publishers, 1999), p. 31.

CHAPTER 11: MARRIAGE FOR THE GLORY OF GOD!

1. Walter Kirn, "Should You Stay Together for the Kids?" *Time* magazine, 25 Sept. 2000. Found on Internet at www.time.com.
2. Ibid.
3. Barna Research Group, "Christians Are More Likely to Experience Divorce Than Are Non-Christians," 21 December 1999.

CHAPTER 12: BUILD YOUR MARRIAGE ON THE ROCK

1. Personal correspondence. Used by permission.
2. Robertson McQuilken address upon his retirement.

F amilyLife has been bringing couples the wonderful news of God's blueprints for marriage since 1976. Today we are strengthening hundreds of thousands of homes in the United States and overseas through:

- ◆ **FamilyLife Marriage Conferences**

- ◆ **I Still Do**™ conferences

- ◆ **HomeBuilders Couples Series**® small-group Bible studies

- ◆ **"FamilyLife Today,"** our nationally syndicated, daily radio program, and several other broadcasts

- ◆ A complete Web site, **www.familylife.com**, featuring daily devotions, conference information, and a wide range of resources for strengthening families

- ◆ Unique marriage and family resources

Through these outreaches, FamilyLife is bringing God's timeless principles home.

FAMILYLIFE™
Bringing Timeless Principles Home

Dennis Rainey, Executive Director
P.O. Box 8220 • Little Rock, Arkansas 72221-8220
1-800-FL-TODAY • www.familylife.com

A division of Campus Crusade for Christ

Get away for a

"Weekend to Remember"

At a FamilyLife
Marriage Conference
you will:

◆ Learn how to com-
municate more
effectively, resolve
conflict, develop
greater sexual inti-
macy, and much
more.

◆ Understand one
another as you dis-
cuss practical proj-
ects as a couple.

◆ Spend valuable
time together and
fall in love all over
again!

It is the most dynamic
and life-changing thing
we've done in our entire
marriage.

Homemaker
Married 7 years

For more information call 1-800-FL-TODAY
or visit www.familylife.com

The Perfect Wedding Gift

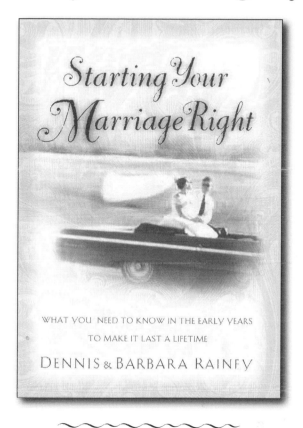

Books offering advice to married couples are hardly new. So what makes *Starting Your Marriage Right* a unique and valuable resource for engaged or recently married couples? This book discusses the issues most couples face in the early years of marriage.

Dennis and Barbara Rainey tackle the all-important "little things" as well as the big issues in marriage: sex, money management, establishing roles, balancing career and marriage, and parenting. Above all, building a stable relationship on the foundation of Jesus Christ is emphasized.

Starting Your Marriage Right is a practical, straightforward manual that can guide couples through the challenges they face as they start their lives together.

Starting Your Marriage Right
ISBN 0-7852-6803-0